THE CRIMEAN OFFENSIVE, 1944

CASEMATE | ILLUSTRATED

CASEMATE | ILLUSTRATED

THE CRIMEAN OFFENSIVE, 1944

THE RUSSIAN BATTLE FOR THE CRIMEA

IAN BAXTER

CASEMATE | ILLUSTRATED

CIS0044

Published in 2025 by
CASEMATE PUBLISHERS
1950 Lawrence Road, Havertown, PA 19083, USA
and
47 Church Street, Barnsley, S70 2AS, UK

Print Edition: ISBN 978-1-63624-435-8
Digital Edition: ISBN 978-1-63624-436-5

Design by Battlefield Design
Maps by Anderson Subtil
Printed and bound in the Czech Republic by FINIDR s.r.o.

CASEMATE PUBLISHERS (US)
Telephone (610) 853-9131
Fax (610) 853-9146
Email: casemate@casematepublishers.com
www.casematepublishers.com

CASEMATE PUBLISHERS (UK)
Telephone (0)1226 734350
Email: casemate@casemateuk.com
www.casemateuk.com

All photos contained in this book are derived from archival sources, including the US National Archives and Records Administration, Library of Congress, Bundesarchiv, the US Military History Institute, and the author's personal collection, unless otherwise noted.

Title page image: A Soviet BM-37 mortarman sights his 82mm weapon.
Contents page image: A Soviet Degtyaryov DP-27/DP-28 machine gunner studies a map.
Contents page map: List from Eastern Europe AMS Topographic Maps. Series N501, U.S. Army Map Service, 1954. Shows mainly the strait and peninsula of Kerch, Taman Peninsula, and Kuban River delta within Krasnodar Krai, as well as parts of the Black Sea and the Sea of Azov.

Acknowledgements: I wish to thank my artist Oliver Missing for his time and expertise in producing some fine and well-detailed illustrations of German and Soviet tanks. Please find Oliver's vast selection of illustrations at his "Engines of WW2" site: www.o5m6.de (founded in 2003). I also wish to thank my Brazilian soldier artist, Renato Dalmaso, who is an illustrator and comic book artist. He works mainly with watercolor and gouache on paper and illustrates the war comic projects *The Elísio: A Journey to Hell and Jambocks*, as well as four comic book albums telling the stories of the Flamengo and São Paulo football clubs. He also works as an illustrator and cover artist for several publications in Europe and Brazil. His email is renatodalmaso@gmail.com.

The Publisher's authorised representative in the EU for product safety is Authorised Rep Compliance Ltd., Ground Floor, 71 Lower Baggot Street, Dublin D02 P593, Ireland.
www.arccompliance.com

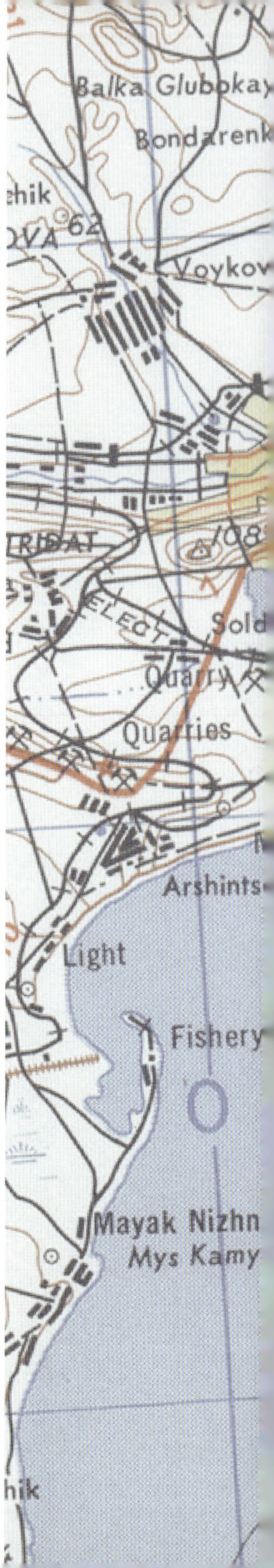

Contents

Timeline of Events

From late November 1943 to early April 1944, the Soviets all but ignored the Crimea. As one senior Soviet officer interrogating a German officer said, "we were in no hurry to take the Crimea. After all, it was our biggest POW cage. The Germans were virtually prisoners on the peninsula since November 1943. They guarded themselves. They supplied themselves. They went on leave and even returned by their own account." This was because of Hitler's irrational infatuation with the Crimea that strategically held little value for the Axis powers. In many respects, as had happened with the Sixth Army at Stalingrad, Hitler also condemned the Seventeenth Army in the Crimea to their fate, even though at the eleventh hour he finally acceded to an evacuation. When the Soviets opened the Crimean offensive on April 8, 1944, around 250,000 German and Romanian troops were facing off against some 460,000 Red Army troops. In the space of a month, the two Axis nations suffered almost 100,000 casualties—many of whom drowned during the evacuation—against the Soviets' 84,000 … and the Crimea was firmly back in Soviet hands.

October 23, 1943: 2nd Ukrainian Front launches an offensive to liberate the Ukrainian industrial centers of Dnepropetrovsk and Dneprodzerzhinsk, advancing 40 miles in a week.

October 25, 1943: Red Army advances to the great bend of the Dnieper River, forcing the German Seventeenth Army to withdraw from the Kuban bridgehead.

October 27, 1943: Seventeenth Army withdraws across the Kerch Strait, and is squeezed into the Perekop Isthmus.

October 28, 1943: Erwin Jaenecke, Seventeenth Army, foresees a major catastrophe and appeals to Hitler to allow his army to undertake a sea evacuation. Hitler forbids any evacuation and orders Jaenecke to hold the Crimea at all costs.

October 28, 1943: Stavka holds a war conference relating to plans to launch a massive offensive, from the Dnieper to the Carpathians, from Polsia to the Black Sea, Western Ukraine, the Crimea, and parts of Romania and Moldova. The Crimea is of strategic importance with four important ports—Feodosiya, Kerch, Sevastopol, and Yevpatoria—for its Black Sea Fleet.

A Red Army PTRD-41 antitank rifle battalion.

October 30, 1943: Stavka directs its attention to recapture the Crimea from the German Seventeenth Army, which is now cut off, with a massive Soviet amphibious landing on the eastern side of the peninsula.

November 1, 1943: Kerch–Eltigen Operation is launched. Soviet troops quickly establish a beachhead and within two days some 4,500 soldiers from the 56th Army's 2nd Guards, 55th Guards, and 32nd Divisions begin pushing inland supported by massed artillery on the Taman Peninsula.

November 7, 1943: The Soviet 383rd Division lands on the Eltigen beachhead in the face of stiff German resistance.

November 11, 1943: 27,700 Soviet reinforcements come ashore at the Yenikale beachhead. The Germans attempt to prevent further reinforcements reaching the Crimea and establish a naval blockade.

December 6, 1943: Romanian 6th Division launches a surprise attack and storms the Eltigen beachhead, killing 1,200 and taking 1,570 Soviet prisoners. The beachhead collapses.

December 11, 1943: Romanian troops capture Mount Mithridates. Soviet troops are withdrawn per the Azov Flotilla to Opasnaya on the Yenikale beachhead.

December 1943–March 1944: A four-month period of inactivity. Seventeenth Army bolsters its defenses with 195,000 troops and establishes staggered, in-depth defensive belts.

March 1944: Stavka revisits the Crimean campaign to capture the peninsula and liberate Sevastopol. 4th Ukrainian Front is allocated the task.

April 7, 1944: General Schörner inspects the Gneisenau Line around Simferopol, pronouncing it solid.

April 8, 1944: 4th Ukrainian Front launches the Crimean offensive to liberate the peninsula. 2nd Guards and 51st Armies deploy troops and armor across the Perekop Isthmus.

April 8/9, 1944: Due to overwhelming Soviet firepower German and Romanian forces begin withdrawing across the Crimea. Schörner tells Chief of the General Staff Kurt Zeitzler that a reluctant retreat to Sevastopol is imminent. Hitler intervenes and forbids outright any retreat, dispatching Zeitzler to army group headquarters to prevent a rout.

April 10, 1944: 4th Ukrainian Front reports that Axis forces are on the run and withdrawing toward the Gneisenau Line.

April 10, 1944: Schörner notifies Hitler that the Gneisenau Line and Sevastopol cannot be held for more than three to four weeks. In anticipation of an evacuation, he has already ordered the navy to send a convoy of boats from Constanta, Romania,

A Soviet 82mm mortar crew prepare their weapon for action.

April 11, 1944: Soviet Separate Coastal Army reaches Simferopol, 37 miles northeast of Sevastopol.

April 12, 1944: The Gneisenau Line is breached in multiple places. Simferopol falls as Soviet armor pours south to take Chisten'koye and Pohtovoye.

April 15, 1944: Seventeenth Army fights a desperate rearguard action outside Sevastopol, with most Axis units retreating toward the port.

April 16, 1944: Hitler instructs Jaenecke that Sevastopol must be held at all costs, but the next day orders all infantry and equipment not required for the defense of the Crimea to be evacuated.

April 28, 1944: As the Crimean situation deteriorates, Jaenecke is ordered to Berchtesgaden where Hitler again promises more reinforcements. An argument ensues and Hitler fires Jaenecke who is replaced by Allmendinger.

May 1, 1944: Red Army Independent Coastal Army is placed under the command of Tolbukhin, who now has 470,000 troops, 600 tanks, and 6,000 guns and mortars at his disposal, all poised to assault the Sevastopol fortified area.

May 5, 1944: Red Army artillery opens a massive bombardment on the German lines. 2nd Guards Army launches a series of attacks in the north that allows Kreizer's 51st Army to attack across the Sapun Hills.

May 6, 1944: German forces sustain some 5,000 casualties, as the defensive ring around Sevastopol is on the point of cracking.

May 8, 1944: The Soviet 63rd Rifle Corps breaks through, dislodging the remaining German defenses. The 10th Rifle Corps pours through the breach to Sevastopol.

May 9, 1944: Schörner sends a message to Hitler: "Request evacuation since further defense of Sevastopol no longer possible." Hitler, worried about another Stalingrad, acquiesces. The chaotic evacuation begins.

May 11, 1944: Relentless Soviet assaults pound Sevastopol. Allmendinger desperately appeals to Admiral Otto Schulz to accelerate the evacuation of the Seventeenth Army, or they will be annihilated.

May 12, 1944: Completion of the evacuation. Of the 64,700 men fighting on the Crimea during the first week of May, 26,700 are left behind to fall into Soviet hands.

Crimea, Ukraine, and southern Russia. (Anderson Subtil)

Introduction: *Barbarossa*

During the early morning of June 22, 1941, the German Army with some 105 infantry divisions and 32 panzer divisions including 3,332 panzers, 7,000 artillery pieces, 60,000 motor vehicles, and 625,000 horses attacked the Soviet Union. This massive army of some three million soldiers was distributed between three army groups: Army Group North, which had assembled its forces in East Prussia on the Lithuanian frontier, Army Group Center, along the 1939 Polish–Soviet frontier, both north and south of Warsaw, and Army Group South, which was deployed along the longest part of the border with Russia attacking formations from central Poland toward the Black Sea.

For Army Group South under Field Marshal Gerd von Rundstedt the main objective was to attack and capture the Ukraine and drive its powerful spearheads southeast into the Crimea. Within a week of the invasion, despite strong Soviet resistance, the city of Lvov was captured by the German Seventeenth Army. What followed was a series of assaults against the fortified areas of Korosten, Novgorod-Volynski, and Letychiv, known as the Stalin Line, that was strung out along 1939 Soviet–Polish border. During early July 1941 the German III Motorized Corps fought several heavy actions in and around Kirponos, and with the arrival

An MG 34 machine gunner looks back at the cameraman as his squad advances with full kit toward the Crimea in the summer of 1941.

In Profile:
German 21cm Mörser M 18/L31 Gunners

21cm Mörser M 18/L31, 624th Heavy Artillery Battalion, Eleventh Army, Severnaya Bay, June 1942

A shirtless gun crew in action. None of the crew wears the standard M40 field blouse with M35 tunic. Nor are they wearing the standard M40 steel helmet, normally standard practice under battle conditions. (Renato Dalmaso)

21cm Mörser M 18/L31, 624th Heavy Artillery Battalion, Eleventh Army, Kerch, June 1942

German gunners in action. They wear the M40 field blouse and M35 tunic with its dark collar. Their field-gray trousers are tucked into their boots. All wear M40 helmets painted in a matt dark gray. (Renato Dalmaso)

The same squad crossing a field, picking their way through what appear to be Soviet foxholes. In the near distance plumes of smoke indicate the battlefield.

A fully laden halftrack hauling a 15cm howitzer on its gun carriage. It generally took a seven-man crew to operate the gun.

of the 11th Panzer Division at Berdichev, the Stalin Line was wrenched open, splitting the Soviet 5th and 6th Armies south of Novgorod-Volynski.

Yet, despite the overwhelming strength of the German attacks through the Ukraine, the Red Army formations, especially mobile units of the Southwestern Front, were able to cause significant damage to Wehrmacht infantry and armor. Nevertheless, although these determined Soviet counterattacks slowed the German advance through the Ukraine, the German Seventeenth Army was able to break through into the Vinnytsia region and drive through to the banks of the Dniester River.

The Red Army attempted to stand firm. But the Southwestern Front, comprising some 50 divisions in six armies, was already in a precarious position with parts of it encircled. It had already thrown its best units into the fray and was using the banks of the Dnieper River as a defensive line. In total the Southwestern Front had some 850,000 soldiers including 90,000 reserves and rearguard units. However, the region it was defending was dominated by the Luftwaffe. Systematically, Red Army positions were bombed from the air while ground formations of the Seventeenth Army began surrounding Soviet units.

While the bulk of Army Group South continued securing and capturing positions deep in the Ukraine before winter set in, it allowed General Erich von Manstein to unleash his Eleventh Army into the Crimean Peninsula. His main objective during September 1941 was to overrun the Crimea and to take the strategic city of Rostov.

On September 24, 1941, Manstein launched a series of concentrated attacks south into the Perekop Isthmus. His aim was to deploy his powerful armored spearheads to Sevastopol and capture the great Soviet naval fortress on the southwestern tip of the peninsula. On September 28 the LIV Corps attacked in the direction of Perekop against six Soviet divisions.

A motorcycle combination passes a convoy of German trucks bound for the Crimea in southern Russia.

Romanian troops advance through Bessarabia in the Ukraine toward the Crimea during the summer of 1941.

Fighting was bitter, and although German and Romanian forces incurred heavy casualties, they successfully captured 10,000 prisoners, 112 tanks, and 135 guns. However, the German success was short-lived as the Soviets counterattacked Manstein's eastern flank. Within days Romanian positions collapsed, and those Axis forces still fighting were in disarray. It appeared that the Soviets had temporarily thwarted the Eleventh Army's advance through the Crimea. Over the next few days German infantry and armor regrouped and between October 5–10 Kleist's First Panzer Army and Manstein's Eleventh Army embarked on a battle of encirclement at the Sea of Azov. Once again, they faced stiff resistance, incurring heavy casualties, which allowed the Soviets three weeks to strengthen Sevastopol and the Crimea as sectors of the front stagnated.

The defense of Sevastopol was supported by the Black Sea Fleet and the Separate Coastal Army. The city garrison was defended by one brigade, three regiments, and 19 battalions of Marine Corps. Strung out across these defenses there were 82 pillboxes with heavy naval guns, 220 machine-gun emplacements, and a multitude of bunker installations. There were

A Red Army T-34 tank crew halting in southern Russia study their maps. Behind them is a column of T-34s.

also 20 miles of antitank ditches dug by Soviet military personnel and civilians. Additional defenses consisted of 30 miles of barbed-wire entanglements and 9,600 mines.

Manstein's Eleventh Army was made up of nine infantry divisions distributed between the LIV Corps and XXX Corps, plus two Romanian rifle corps, and various supporting elements including 150 panzers and several hundred aircraft. The army also boasted heavy artillery and mortar battalions.

On October 30, 1941, Manstein's forces launched a series of attacks against Sevastopol and quickly secured the Balaklava Hills. He then dispatched panzer and infantry formations at speed toward the city from the north, northeast, and east. However, the Germans were halted and driven back but did manage to encircle the city. The Soviets were determined to hold on to Sevastopol and began reinforcing its garrison from the sea. Most of the reinforcement troops it received had been embarked from Odessa.

Over the next week Manstein began bringing up additional artillery to bombard the fortress. Heavy mortar and artillery fire pounded the Soviet positions while 60,000 Axis soldiers launched another attack. However, following almost two weeks of continuous fighting, Manstein was forced to call off the attack. Instead, he changed tactics and launched attacks against the enclave's southern flank. Once again, he failed to subdue Soviet resistance. On December 4 the local Soviet command reported that Fortress Sevastopol had been reestablished. With the German attacks blunted, Manstein ordered his largest artillery piece, the 80cm "*Schwerer Gustav*," brought up.

Five days later, December 17, six German infantry divisions and two Romanian brigades with 1,275 guns and mortars, 150 tanks, and 300 aircraft launched another protracted attack.

Soviet infantry move forward toward the battlefront supported by heavy KV-1 tanks. These tanks were known for their heavy armored protection during the initial stages of the war on the Eastern Front and were used extensively by the Red Army.

Four days later, German units managed to break through Soviet defenses within a mile of Severnaya Bay. A Soviet counterattack was immediately undertaken by the newly arrived 79th Independent Naval Infantry Brigade. As a result, the German attack failed.

By the first week of January 1942 Soviet resistance had further strengthened, with the Red Army launching their own winter offensive. Across the Axis front Soviet forces forced several of Manstein's formations to withdraw. While German commanders in the field tried to hold their lines on the Kerch Peninsula, the Red Army landed some 42,000

An MG 34 machine gunner has adapted his weapon for action inside a captured Soviet bunker in the Crimea, early October 1941.

troops belonging to the 44th and 51st Armies near Theordosia and Feodosiya. The Soviet amphibious assault was an attempt to regain the initiative on the Crimea and assist Soviet land forces fighting in and around Sevastopol.

Throughout January and February 1942, the Germans persisted in trying to capture Sevastopol, but Soviet defenses held firm. What followed were weeks of German attacks and Soviet counterattacks with no resolution. On April 9 the Red Army opened a powerful counterattack with six divisions and 160 tanks. However, despite a promising start, the Germans caused significant losses.

On May 8, the German Eleventh Army then launched their own offensive, codenamed *Unternehmen Trappenjagd*. The plan was to drive Red Army divisions back from the Kerch area and resume the assault on Sevastopol. In front of Manstein's forces were 17 infantry divisions and several independent brigades. The Germans had seven infantry divisions and a panzer division. Roughly a third of the German force was Romanian. Following several determined attacks supported by artillery, mortars, and the Luftwaffe from the north, the Eleventh Army managed to smash through the enemy lines and force the Red Army back to the Kerch Strait. Fighting continued to rage, but by May 18, the overwhelmed Soviet forces in the area surrendered and 170,000 prisoners were taken by the Germans. To avoid complete annihilation the remnants of the Soviet land forces in the Crimea then withdrew by sea. The only land mass still not captured was the besieged city of Sevastopol. To eliminate this resistance the Germans brought in several heavy guns, together with massed artillery. Bunker-busting guns such as the massive 60cm Mörser "*Karl*" Gerät 040 siege mortar gun were transported to the Sevastopol area for the assault. Even the massive *Schwerer Gustav* that required 250 men to assemble the gun and 2,500 personnel to lay rail track and dig

Soviet troops charge in the snow against German positions in the Crimea, winter 1941. One soldier appears to have been hit leaving his trench.

German troops including an MG 34 machine gunner pose in a dugout in the Crimea during winter operations.

Captured Soviet soldiers being rounded up in a wooded area.

A German heavy-caliber gun elevated in preparation for a fire mission against Sevastopol.

embankments was used for the siege. It took 4,000 men five weeks to prepare the gun and 500 men to fire it.

While the siege guns were being prepared and moved into place, on May 21 the Luftwaffe launched a massive bombardment on Sevastopol. This was followed for two weeks by concentrated shelling by artillery and heavy mortars. By early June German troops had managed to break through the second line of Soviet defenses and storm and secure vital

A German 15cm howitzer crew block their ears as the weapon is fired, April 1942.

The massive *Schwerer Gustav*. The Heavy Artillery Unit (E) 672 moved this gun by train through southern Russia and reached the Perekop Isthmus in early March 1942. With its monstrous 80cm caliber, at the time this was the largest gun in the world. It was used against Sevastopol in June 1942.

Soviet soldiers being shown how to strip and assemble the PTRD-41 antitank rifle, June 1942.

German infantry sit poised inside a captured Soviet trench before resuming their attack, Sevastopol, June 1942.

areas around the city. With the Soviet defenses breached, Manstein launched *Unternehmen Störfang* (Sturgeon Catch). This operation was primarily to prevent the Soviets supplying Sevastopol from the sea, and would allow Manstein's forces to capture the city without spending weeks or even months battering the fortress into submission.

For the operation the Germans committed the LIV Corps supported by the XXX Corps. Each German formation was supported by a smaller Romanian corps. The attack was fierce and constant and by June 16 the outer defensive rings of the city had been breached. However, heavy resistance continued despite high Soviet losses. Manstein could see his attacks faltering and on June 28 ordered an amphibious crossing of Severnaya Bay to outflank the Soviet defensive lines. Bitter fighting raged and German losses mounted, thwarting further attacks in front of Sevastopol.

Over the coming days and weeks Sevastopol was pounded by relentless German shelling and countless Luftwaffe attacks. Soviet forces fought to the grim death to defend the besieged city, but slowly and methodically Soviet defenses were destroyed by the heavy guns and consequently troops were forced out into the open. Thousands were killed before the fortress finally fell on July 3. Two more Soviet armies on the Crimea had been annihilated and 90,000 prisoners taken, along with 467 guns, 758 mortars, 26 tanks, 141 aircraft, and 155 antitank guns. Hitler, overjoyed at hearing the news, telephoned Manstein and praised him as "the Conqueror of Sevastopol and the Crimea," informing him of his promotion to *Generalfeldmarshall.*

Red Army infantry, especially penal battalions, charged German lines in massed attacks. This photograph shows a Soviet unit charging a German defensive line and a Soviet soldier getting hit by mortar fire.

German soldiers at one of the knocked-out Gorky I naval batteries at Sevastopol.

Although the surrounding caves around the peninsula and other pockets of resistance held out for several weeks, Sevastopol and the Crimea was finally conquered by the Germans in the summer of 1942.

A German 10.5cm gun crew overlooking Sevastopol.

A German sailor poses on one of the captured Soviet naval guns at Sevastopol.

The Maxim Gorky I naval gun armored turret located east of Ljabimorka and north of Severnaya Bay that formed Sevastopol's harbor.

The captured Maxim Gorky I naval gun, with its twin 305mm gun turret. The Maxim Gorky II was located on the seaward cliffs southwest of Sevastopol.

Another view of the captured Maxim Gorky I naval gun. Damaged by the *Schwerer Gustav*, but still able to fire, it was only finally knocked out of action by German assault engineers on June 17.

Soviet POWs following their defeat in the Crimea.

Dejected, wounded Red Army POWs in the rubble in Sevastopol. It is unlikely that any would survive the war.

A Wehrmacht soldier looks out across the battle-ravaged bay following the capture of Sevastopol in July 1942.

In Profile:
Soviet Riflemen

386th Rifle Division, Siege of Sevastopol, May 1942

Soviet riflemen dismount from a T-34 tank near Sevastopol. The aim of German Operation *Störfang* was to eliminate Soviet forces defending Sevastopol and capture the port. A dismounted Soviet infantryman has just been shot. (Renato Dalmaso)

161st Rifle Regiment, 95th Rifle Division, Siege of Sevastopol, June 1942

This rifleman is armed with a PPSh-41 submachine gun. He wears the Red Army *pilotka* cap with metal star and a *plaschpalatka* poncho over his standard service uniform. (Renato Dalmaso)

Battle of the Dnieper, August 26–December 23, 1943

Following the success of capturing the Crimea, the peninsula came under Nazi military administration in what was officially termed *Generalbezirk Krym-Taurien*, an administrative division of Reichskommissariat Ukraine. The whole of the Crimea was subordinated to a military administration and subjected to harsh German control, including plans for future colonization by *Volksdeutschen* and ruthless policies with extreme measures of cleansing Jews, communists, and uncooperative Slavs from the peninsula. For the next two years, the Crimea would suffer brutal repression under the Germans.

A column of Soviet ISU-152s advances to the front. This self-propelled gun was nicknamed "*Zveroboy*," or Beast Killer. The vehicle was built in direct response to the large German tanks and self-propelled guns entering service in 1942 and 1943 such as the Tiger and Panther.

Red Army riflemen charge a German position supported by an SU-76 light self-propelled gun.

An SU-76 advances through a village toward the Dnieper River in 1943. While the vehicle's armor was thin and its open-top crew compartment made it vulnerable to antitank weapons and grenades, it had good maneuverability on the battlefield.

German troops interrogate a very young captured Soviet soldier.

Elsewhere on the Eastern Front the Red Army continued resisting. Following the loss of Stalingrad in January 1943, German forces in southern Russia were thrown into disarray. Army Group A was assigned to hold the Kuban bridgehead to protect the Crimea. Defenses were erected known as the *Gotenkopf-Stellung* or "Goth's head position" where a staggering 20 divisions were assembled comprising some 400,000 troops in the Kuban and in the Crimea. So concerned were the Germans about losing positions on the lower Dnieper that between March and August 1943 large quantities of material were transported from the Crimea to Kuban to bolster their defenses. In total, some 337,353 tons of supplies, 6,365 troops, 2,566 horses, 1,099 motor vehicles, 534 horse-drawn vehicles, and 197 heavy guns were shipped.

In the spring of 1943, the Red Army launched a series of attacks in the south. Army Group A was ordered to secure the lower Dnieper River line and stall the advance of the Soviet Southern Front. Over the weeks and months to come Army Group A fought a series of hard-pressed battles to slow the enemy from breaking out west and entering the Crimea.

By the summer of 1943 the German war machine was already on the brink of beginning its slow withdrawal back toward the Reich. Southern Russia bore the heaviest show of force by the Red Army comprising the Voronezh and Steppe Fronts. During the second half of 1943 the Germans were forced to strengthen their lines and defend while the Soviets went over onto the offensive.

A Soviet 82mm mortar crew prepare to fire.

A German Nashorn tanker eating a slice of bread smiles for camera while riding to the front. These vehicles were issued to the heavy antitank battalions and mounted a variant of the 8.8cm Pak 43. The vehicle performed well in the summer of 1943 and was able to engage the enemy at long distances.

In August 1943 the First Panzer Army was given the daunting task of defending positions along the River Donets. Throughout the remainder of August and into September, due to high losses, mechanical breakdowns, and the lack of replacements, Wehrmacht and Waffen-SS divisions could only muster 1,000 panzers operationally in southern Russia. Consequently, the Germans could not hold the front for any appreciable length of time. By October Army Group South had been forced to withdraw some 150 miles along its entire front. In some areas the front was in danger of collapsing entirely. Manstein, who in March 1943 had been appointed commander in chief of Army Group South, appealed

A dusty and disheveled German MG 42 machine gunner.

A German soldier surveys a knocked-out 1943 model T-34 tank.

A familiar scene in the summer of 1943: Red Army troops supported by armor charging German lines.

An SU-152 advances at speed along a typical dusty road to the front.

Closeup of a Soviet SU-122 self-propelled howitzer. The number 122 in the vehicle's designation represents the caliber of the main armament: a 122mm M-30S howitzer.

A young Soviet soldier takes aim with his PPSh submachine gun that fired the 7.62x25mm Tokarev round.

Soviet pilots enjoy a pause during operations in the summer of 1943.

A Soviet SU-85 self-propelled gun fords the Dnieper River in August 1943. This vehicle entered service that month and was used throughout the remainder of the war.

A Soviet artillery crew manhandle a 76mm M1942 (ZiS-3) divisional field gun across the Dnieper River.

Soviet soldiers on the Dnieper River armed with the Maxim 1910/30 machine gun.

A staged photograph of Soviet troops manning a PTRD-41 single-shot antitank rifle in the summer of 1943. The other primary Soviet antitank rifle was the PTRS-41, capable of semi-automatic fire.

A Soviet SU-85 self-propelled gun advances at speed to the front.

Two Soviet snipers concealed in brush. Soviet snipers, many of whom were women, were a constant menace to the Germans and many soldiers were killed.

to Hitler to withdraw his formations across the River Dnieper, which was regarded as a natural obstacle of defense in the Ukraine. What followed was a desperate retreat to cross the Dnieper while several Wehrmacht units were left behind to take up positions defending towns and cities to slow the furious advance of the Red Army. As the Germans withdrew, they implemented a "scorched earth" policy to destroy all resources that might be of use to

In foul weather, German troops withdraw across a tributary of the Dnieper River, October 1943.

Ukrainian women forced into digging trenches and antitank defenses west of the Dnieper River, October 1943. Three German soldiers appear to be assisting.

Winter-clad German gunners fire a 7.5cm GebG 36 artillery piece. This was a light gun which German mountain troops used but which was also found in conventional German infantry units.

the Red Army. Thankfully for the Axis forces, the Soviet advance slowed, allowing troops and armor to scramble across the Dnieper. The operation by Manstein to save Army Group South from annihilation was one of his major military successes, but gone were the days of bold Wehrmacht offensives.

The Red Army, however, was determined to advance to the Dnieper, cross and recover all the lost territory west of the river, including wheeling south and taking back the Crimea. Soviet armies of the 1st, 2nd, and 3rd Belorussian, and 4th Ukrainian Fronts stretched from Smolensk to the Sea of Azov and comprised 2,650,000 troops with 51,000 guns and mortars, 2,400 tanks, and 2,850 aircraft. This concentration of firepower was formidable. Throughout September and October 1943, the Belorussian and Ukrainian Fronts systemically attacked German blocking formations that were defending west and east of the Dnieper. Along great stretches of the river German formations were unable to build adequate defensive positions in time, with numerous sectors having no depth. Consequently, Red Army divisions were able to take advantage of German weak spots and undertake several assault crossings.

By late September bridgeheads had been established near Dneprodzerzhinsk and Kremenchuk. On October 4 the whole of Army Group A, which had been defending positions in the South including the Kuban bridgehead, was organized into two field armies, the Sixth and Seventeenth, with a total of five corps. These forces were allocated purely defensive

A whitewashed heavy German 21cm Mörser howitzer. These massive guns were used by independent artillery battalions and batteries.

German ski troops on a reconnaissance mission.

tasks: to defend their lines against the advancing Soviet juggernaut. Within two weeks, the 2nd Ukrainian Front successfully crossed the Dnieper River, forcing German divisions to withdraw. Over the next days and weeks more bridgeheads were established that allowed the Red Army to pour significant numbers of men and quantities of material into western Ukraine. What followed was the Dnepropetrovsk Offensive Operation, part of several sub-operations launched by the Red Army to retake the lower Dnieper. The operation's aim was to destroy German forces still resisting in the Dneprodzerzhinsk and the Krivoi Rog

German troops wearing the familiar winter reversibles packing their gear and loading their kit onto sleds during the Seventeenth Army's withdrawal in the winter of 1943.

Two winter-clad German soldiers pose next to their Kubelwagen.

area north of the Crimean Peninsula. Some 100,000 Soviet troops with 2,000 artillery pieces and mortars supported by tanks and self-propelled vehicles prepared for the operation. Against this Soviet force was Manstein's Army Group South, comprising 25,000 soldiers of the First Panzer Army supported by some 50 panzers and several hundred artillery pieces and mortars.

On October 23, 1943, the 2nd Ukrainian Front launched

Even by 1943 German soldiers on the Eastern Front had adapted a variety of clothing to keep warm. Both soldiers here are wearing the single-piece snow apron over their service uniform.

Sparsely clad German soldiers trudge through the snow during a retreat.

Soviet troops overrun a German trench during winter operations in late 1943. A dead German soldier is in the foreground.

A Soviet soldier clambers onto the front of an ISU-152 bound for the front during operations in late 1943. The vehicle displays an effective ad hoc camouflage pattern.

A German 15cm howitzer crew prepare to open fire. Snow chains are attached to the howitzer's wheels.

In a dug-in German defensive position west of the Dnieper is a well-concealed 15cm howitzer.

its offensive. The speed and power of the attack was so overwhelming that within two days the Red Army had liberated the industrial centers of Dnepropetrovsk and Dneprodzerzhinsk. Within a week the Soviet advance had penetrated the German lines by almost 40 miles, sending German troops reeling back across the western plains of the Ukraine. The speed of the Soviet offensive meant that the First Panzer Army holding positions along the southeastern sector of the great bend of the Dnieper was no longer able to protect the Seventeenth Army. Already the Seventeenth Army was facing relentless enemy firepower and had slowly withdrawn from the Kuban bridgehead, which was a heavily fortified line of defenses and used by the Wehrmacht to carry out renewed attacks toward the oilfields of the Caucasus.

Defending the bridgehead the Seventeenth Army comprised the "Wetzel Group" that consisted of X Army Corps under the command of General Wilhelm Wetzel, XLIV Army Corps, and XLIX Army Corps, plus a Romanian corps; altogether some six German and two Romanian divisions dug in along the 100-mile front from Novorossiysk to Kurchanskaya. However, although these defenses were considerably fortified, the Seventeenth Army lacked meaningful reinforcements and was short of weaponry and armor. The combined German and Romanian forces that were defending the line totaled some 200,000 men, but they were up against a much superior enemy army totaling a combined strength of more than 350,000 men. Along the Kuban bridgehead the Seventeenth Army was hard-pressed to maintain its defenses between the Black Sea and the Sea of Azov. Pressure on its positions was made considerably worse as the Red Army launched a series of attacks on the lower Dnieper River. Along the Kuban bridgehead units of the Seventeenth Army were attacked relentlessly by both ground and air attacks. The weight of Soviet firepower was so overwhelming that General Erwin Jaenecke, commander of the Seventeenth Army, ordered

Soviet artillery crew prepare their 76mm M1942 (ZiS-3) divisional gun for action in the winter of 1943/44.

An SU-85 on an icy road. Though powerful and effective, crews found that its 85mm gun was inadequate in penetrating the armor of the larger German armored fighting vehicles. It would be replaced by the SU-100.

his men to withdraw from the bridgehead or face total annihilation. Inexorably divisions of the Seventeenth Army withdrew across the Kerch Strait into the Crimea, fanatically trying to hold back the overwhelming might of the Red Army. However, it was pushed back and squeezed through a narrow tract of land from the Ukraine into the Perekop Isthmus into the Crimea. This action cut off the land-based connection of the Seventeenth Army through the Perekop Isthmus. Consequently, the German Army was all but cut off with no escape except by sea.

Jaenecke could see a major catastrophe looming and appealed to Hitler, requesting that his army undertake a sea evacuation. Hitler, however, forbade any seaborne evacuation as he was concerned that the Soviets would use the Crimean Peninsula to launch air attacks against Romanian oil refineries. Hitler also wanted to retain the Crimea because of the iron and manganese mines at Krivoi Rog and Nikopol. He was well aware that the Soviets were determined to retake the Crimea at whatever cost. To save the Crimea from being overrun and hold back Red Army forces in the lower Dnieper, he gave General Ferdinand Schörner, his ruthless defense expert and fanatical Nazi, command of XXXX Panzer Corps. Although the line of defense boasted good field fortifications, with floodplains and watercourses to hinder enemy assaults, Schörner's units were thinly spread and lacked sufficient armor and weaponry to sustain themselves for any length of time. However, Schörner was also relying on the harsh winter weather to assist in slowing the Red Army. Yet, despite his audacious plans to help relieve the southern bend of the Dnieper and the Crimea, the Seventeenth Army was already cut off on the peninsula.

Stavka, the Russian high command, had anticipated success in the area and drawn up plans to launch a massive offensive aimed at the southern part of the Ukraine that encompassed a huge area from the Dnieper to the Carpathians, from Polsia to the Black Sea, Western Ukraine, the Crimea, and the areas of Romania and Moldova. For Stavka the Crimea was of strategic importance. It comprised the four important ports of Feodosiya, Kerch, Sevastopol, and Yevpatoria that would secure the Black Sea Fleet in the central and western Black Sea.

This planned offensive owed much to the defeat of German and Romanian forces on the eastern side of the Kerch Strait that separated the Crimea from Kuban. With the German Seventeenth Army now isolated in the Crimea, it could still nevertheless be supplied by sea. The Seventeenth Army comprised V Corps in the north, XLIX Mountain Corps defending the Perekop Isthmus, and a Romanian Mountain Corps in the southern and southeastern parts of the Crimea. These formations were supported by numerous flak and artillery troops and 45 assault guns.

To prepare for what Stavka would call the Crimean Offensive Operation, they planned a large-scale amphibious landing on the eastern and western sides of the Crimea. This would be known as the Kerch–Eltingen Offensive Operation.

A Soviet antitank rifle position. The crew await advancing enemy armor.

In Profile:
Wehrmacht MG 42 Machine Gunner and Panzerfaust Operator

MG 42 Machine Gunner, 371st Infantry Division, Fourth Panzer Army, Dnieper River, July 1943

A German machine gunner, his weapon shouldered. He wears the M43 field cap and M35 field-gray tunic. (Renato Dalmaso)

Panzerfaust Operator, 98th Infantry Division, Seventeenth Army, Kuban Bridgehead, September 1943

This soldier is armed with the deadly Panzerfaust single-shot, portable antitank weapon, as well as a captured Soviet PPSh-41 submachine gun. He wears an M43 field-gray tunic with marching boots and gaiters. (Renato Dalmaso)

Soviet Order of Battle, August–December 1943

Central Front

known as the Belorussian Front after October 20, 1943, commanded by Konstantin Rokossovsky

- 2nd Tank Army (Aleksei Rodin/Semyon Bogdanov since September)
- 9th Tank Corps (Hryhoriy Rudchenko, Boris Bakharov)
- 60th Army (Ivan Chernyakhovsky)
- 13th Army (Nikolay Pukhov)
- 65th Army (Pavel Batov)
- 61st Army (Pavel Belov)
- 48th Army (Prokofy Romanenko)
- 70th Army (Ivan Galanin/Vladimir Sharapov September/October/Aleksei Grechkin since October)
- 16th Air Army (Sergei Rudenko)

Voronezh Front

known as the 1st Ukrainian Front after October 20, 1943, commanded by Nikolai Vatutin

- 3rd Guards Tank Army (Pavel Rybalko)
- 1st Tank Army (Mikhail Katukov)
- 4th Guards Tank Corps (Pavel Poluboyarov)
- 1st Guard Cavalry Corps (Viktor Baranov)
- 5th Guards Army (Aleksei Zhadov)
- 4th Guards Army (Grigory Kulik/Aleksei Zygin KIA/Ivan Galanin)
- 6th Guards Army (Ivan Chistyakov)
- 38th Army (Nikandr Chibisov/Kirill Moskalenko since October)
- 47th Army (Pavel Korzun/Filipp Zhmachenko September/October/Vitaliy Polenov since October)
- 27th Army (Sergei Trofimenko)
- 52nd Army (Konstantin Koroteev)
- 2nd Air Army (Stepan Krasovsky)

Steppe Front

known as the 2nd Ukrainian Front after October 20, 1943, commanded by Ivan Konev

Southwestern Front

known as the 3rd Ukrainian Front after October 20, 1943, commanded by Rodion Malinovsky

Southern Front

known as the 4th Ukrainian Front after October 20, 1943, commanded by Fyodor Tolbukhin

German Order of Battle, August–December 1943

Luftflotte 2

- selected units (Wolfram Freiherr von Richthofen)

Army Group South (Ukraine) (Erich von Manstein)

- Fourth Panzer Army (Hermann Hoth)
- First Panzer Army (Eberhard von Mackensen)
- Eighth Army (Otto Wohler)
- Sixth Army (Karl-Adolf Hollidt) (transferred to Army Group A)

Luftflotte 4 (Wolfram Freiherr von Richthofen/Otto Deßloch since September)

Army Group Center (Gunther von Kluge)

- Second Army (Walter Weiß, took no part in the Dnieper battle after October 3)

In Profile:
Soviet Maxim Machine Gunner and 82-BM-37 Mortar Crew

Maxim M1910 Machine Gunner, 5th Guards Tank Army, Perekop Isthmus, October 1943

A Red Army machine gunner and his number two in action. T-34 tanks support the attack. Both soldiers wear the standard infantryman's greatcoat and, on their head, the *ushanka*. (Renato Dalmaso)

82-BM-37 Mortar Crew, 27th Army, Dnieper River, September 1943

A Red Army battery officer signals his mortar crew to open fire. They all wear the summer tunic and trousers complete with *pilotka* hat with Soviet badge. (Renato Dalmaso)

Kerch–Eltigen Operation, November 1943

Following the successful operations on the lower Dnieper River and breaching it in several areas that saw Soviet troops gaining a foothold on the western bank, Stavka now directed its attention to recapturing the Crimea from the German Seventeenth Army that was now cut off. The plan was for a massive Soviet amphibious landing on the eastern side of the Crimean Peninsula. The attack was in preparation for its Crimean Offensive Operation. Erwin Jaenecke, commander of the Seventeenth Army, was under no illusions as to the severity of the situation. His forces were totally isolated, and he knew if he did not evacuate his troops by sea another catastrophe with the same magnitude as Stalingrad could.

The Soviets, however, wanted to launch their amphibious operation as quickly as possible before the Seventeenth Army could prepare any type of evacuation. For the landings, the 4th Ukrainian Front prepared the 18th Army and 56th Army including the Black Sea

German troops in the Crimea wearing the familiar winter reversibles white-side out.

A German officer wearing a greatcoat and whitewashed M1935 steel helmet with some of his troops.

Fleet and Azov Flotilla. The former comprised the battleship *Sevastopol*, four cruisers (two *Kirov*-class—*Molotov* and *Voroshilov* and *Krasniy Krim* and *Krasniy Kavkaz*), destroyer leader *Kharkov*, five modern and three older destroyers, and 29 submarines. The Azov Flotilla comprised two torpedo speedboats, 15 gunboats, three escort vessels, and eight

A German Nebelwerfer rocket launcher positioned near the Kerch Strait. It is draped with straw, either as camouflage or protection from the elements.

Winter-clad German troops march through a Crimean village.

minesweepers. It also included a battalion of marine infantry, an infantry battalion, and four antiaircraft batteries.

Despite the postponement of the main seaborne operation due to bad weather and rough seas, the Red Army did manage to launch various naval craft during the night of October 30, 1943. The assault was messy due to high waves and darkness, but the boats did manage to force a risky landing with the 318th Division of the 18th Army and the 386th Naval Battalion along the shores at Eltigen on the eastern side of the Crimea on November 1. Defending the beach was a motley assortment of Romanian units dug in along the shore plus various mortar and machine-gun positions set up, including old 7.5cm le.IG 18 infantry guns that were supposed to repel any enemy attack.

When the Soviets landed, they immediately stormed the Romanian positions under a hail of fire. However, the Soviets were fighting poorly trained and poorly equipped troops whose defensive emplacements were often crude and easily overrun. The Romanians were quite unprepared for the Soviet attack. Along most of the coastline at Eltigen they were simply brushed aside and annihilated. Romanian survivors recalled that they were caught completely off guard. There was also no reassurance from their commanders either, as most of them had already deserted the front and fled inland, thus the leaderless Romanians were unable to mount any organized defense. In total confusion, hundreds of disheartened and frightened troops retreated to avoid annihilation. By early afternoon Soviet forces had made considerable progress and had battered the Romanian defensive positions into submission

Two photographs taken in sequence showing a German antitank gun position at the front. The winter whitewash provides excellent camouflage.

A German soldier surveys the terrain through a pair of trench binoculars at a forward observation post.

Two German soldiers in winter reversibles share a cigarette in the snow.

German troops take a break on their sled.

German troops relax while two play accordions.

A German soldier armed with a captured Soviet PPSh-41 submachine gun.

on the flat, grassy, rocky ground behind the beach until parts of the front collapsed in confusion.

On the first day the Soviets established a small beachhead and within two days some 4,500 soldiers from the 56th Army's 2nd Guards Division, 55th Guards Division, and 32nd Division began pushing inland supported by massed artillery from positions on the Taman Peninsula. Yet, despite the initial success of the Red Army landings, some Romanian forces regrouped and consolidated their lines of defense. The 3rd Gebirgsjäger Division, V Corps, repulsed further attacks and Soviet losses began to mount. Over the next few days fighting intensified, with the Red Army still unable to completely subdue the Romanian defenses.

German troops transporting ammunition cases on sleds towed by horses.

Two German infantrymen inside one of the numerous trenches dug along the front.

On November 7, the Soviets landed further reinforcements from the 383rd Division. Although these forces, consisting mainly of the 117th Guards Regiment, were able to reinforce troops on the Eltigen beachhead, they were also continuously repulsed. Four days later more reinforcements were rushed to the area, with 27,700 troops landed on the Yenikale beachhead. The Germans, however, wanting to prevent more reinforcements reaching the Crimea, established a naval blockade around the landings and beachheads with minesweepers and other craft from the 3rd Minensuch-

A typical German MG 34 machine-gun position in a solid bunker.

Soviet engineers bring artillery and horses to the beachhead on makeshift landing craft. The Soviet amphibious attack at Kerch was a precursor to the Crimean offensive.

Soviet engineers constructing a jetty of logs strapped together to move men and materials from the boats and landing craft.

Two photographs taken in sequence of Soviet troops during the amphibious landing, holding onto each other due to the strength of the tide.

Red Army troops arrive at the beachhead.

Soviet troops negotiate a quagmire following the landing across the Kerch Strait near Sivash. The Sivash is a large area of shallow lagoons on the western edge of the Sea of Azov separated from the sea by the narrow Arabat Spit. This large area borders the northeastern coast of the Crimean Peninsula.

Soviet troops trudge through the icy lagoons of the Sivash.

Soviet troops pull an artillery piece through the muddy lagoons of the Sivash, December 1943.

Red Army troops sit round a fire cooking their food. One reads out a newspaper for his comrades.

Two Soviet female personnel armed with the DP-27 light machine gun smile for the camera. This 47-round weapon was the most widely used light machine gun used by the Soviets during the war.

A truck with fresh-faced Soviet infantry bound for the front. Many of the men riding on it are armed with the PPSh-41 submachine gun.

a result, to help repel the Soviets the Romanian 3rd Gebirgsjäger Division was ordered to counterattack. Over the course of the next few days in cold, driving sleet, heavy fighting continued, and losses mounted on both sides. The Soviets' reserves had almost gone and those troops fighting to contain their positions were at the end of their endurance. In many cases Soviet wounded were simply abandoned as their positions buckled under the Romanian onslaught. The Soviets showed great fortitude, but because they were in dire need of weapons and manpower, they could not sustain themselves on the battlefield for any length of time. Consequently, on December 11, the Romanians successfully captured Mount Mithridates. Those Soviet soldiers that had not been killed or captured managed to escape and were evacuated to Opasnaya in the Yenikale beachhead by one of the ships from the Azov Flotilla.

With the Soviets unable to sustain their positions at Eltigen, they now began concentrating their efforts towards reinforcing the Yenikale beachhead. During early December, while the Romanians were successfully counterattacking, the Soviets had begun shipping more men and material to the beachhead. Some 75,000 troops, together with 187 mortars, 882 guns, 764 trucks, 128 tanks, and 10,000 tons of munitions and material were landed. Yet, despite these reinforcements, Stavka regarded this operation as a mere token and a temporary solution. For the moment the Red Army was busily embroiled driving its armies across the Dnieper River west through the Ukraine, clearing vast areas of territory from the retreating Wehrmacht. Plans for the capture of the Crimea were postponed to the spring of 1944.

As for the German Seventeenth Army, its divisions were able to operate effectively and build its reserves from supplies being shipped in from the Black Sea, but it was obvious that being cut off from the mainland and being supplied by sea was only a short-term solution.

A Soviet soldier next to his bunker repairs one of his boots.

Soviet POWs trudge through the snow following their capture after intensive fighting near Kerch.

In Profile: Heer and Red Army Infantrymen

German Infantrymen, 73rd Infantry Division, Seventeenth Army, the Crimea, December 1943

These infantrymen wear one-piece winter-white blankets over their standard-issue gray uniforms. The soldier on the right is armed with the Karabiner 98k bolt-action rifle. He wears a black leather belt with ammunition pouches, the M38 field cap, and holds his M35 steel helmet which has a canvas winter-white cover. The soldier on the left wears mittens and the German fur cap. He also holds an M35 steel helmet. (Renato Dalmaso)

Red Army Officer, 383rd Division, Eltigen Beachhead, December 1943

This officer, armed with a PPSh-41, wears a greatcoat and *ushanka* fur hat. The winter coat was very warm, thick, and impermeable. Around his waist he wears the infantry leather belt. Although obscured by his greatcoat, he will be wearing long, black leather marching boots. (Renato Dalmaso)

In Profile:
Pz.Kpfw. IVs Ausf. G & Ausf. H

Pz.Kpfw. IV Ausf. H, December 1944

To prepare the defense on the Crimea the Germans created mobile reserves that comprised a motley collection of panzer units, assault-gun battalions, and motorized antitank units. This panzer, unit unknown, has been liberally applied with winter whitewash over its summer camouflage colors. Its *schürzen* or side skirts are intact and show no unit insignia other than its black cross painted on the side of the turret. (Oliver Missing)

Pz.Kpfw. IV Ausf. G, December 1944

This panzer, unit unknown, has no *schürzen* or side skirts and has been whitewashed over its summer sand-colored camouflage scheme. It was one of several vehicles in an ad hoc group of panzers used for the defense of the Crimea. (Oliver Missing)

Hiatus, December 1943–March 1944

Ever since the German war machine occupied the Crimea in 1942, Hitler had been obsessed with the peninsula. In his eyes the Crimea was the gateway to the Black Sea and the Romanian oilfields, on which his armies depended, and that were within distance of Crimean airbases. Hitler often referred to the Crimea as an "unsinkable aircraft carrier," and for that reason he said it was imperative to hold on to the peninsula at all costs.

However, by late 1943 with the Red Army advancing through the Ukraine, the Crimea was under direct threat of invasion. Luckily for the Germans the front along the Dnieper River south to the Crimean Peninsula had stagnated due to the harsh winter conditions. While this gave time for German forces in the Ukraine to recoup their massive losses, the Seventeenth Army in the Crimea continued to prepare its defensive positions with its 195,000 troops. Supplies were continuously mounting with German and Romanian convoys shipping weaponry and ammunition from Romania to Sevastopol.

The staggered German defense in the Crimea was manned in numerous defensive belts composed of antitank strongholds, including an extensive network of antitank obstacles. The strength of the German defenses varied significantly. Some were no more than a series of MG 42 or MG 34 machine-gun nests, while others comprised Flak and Pak strongpoints surrounded by a maze of trenches, bunkers, and mortar pits. The 8.8cm Paks were used in both aerial and ground roles. Parts of the front were mined and protected by barbed-wire barriers.

However, the Seventeenth Army was overstretched, undermanned and undergunned. Cut off, it was only a matter of time before the Red Army launched an offensive against the Crimea, predicted to come in the spring. By March 1944, the Soviets had already assembled a force of some 470,000 troops for the offensive.

The Crimea was regarded as a formidable barrier to any invader. Undertaking any type of invasion from the mainland, the Germans knew that an attacker had three possible options. The Perekop Isthmus was five miles wide and was the most likely. Luckily for the Wehrmacht old 1941 Soviet defensive works stretched across the isthmus and German engineers were set to work to make them battleworthy. Another route that the Red Army could take was east of Perekop across the Sivash marshlands. However, this tract of land was deemed difficult, and the Germans doubted any type of attack would be launched there. Nevertheless, sappers were sent to the Sivash where defensive works were undertaken.

In Profile:
General Erwin Jaenecke

Erwin Jaenecke had a successful military career as a commander. He first served in 1939 during operations in Poland and then in Belgium and France. In Russia he was appointed commander of the 389th Infantry Division and later the IV Army Corps. As with many commanders in the field, the general oversaw several brutal actions in suppressing the local population and murdering Soviet POWs. In late 1942/early 1943 Jaenecke was wounded at Stalingrad and was one of the last officers flown out before the doomed city fell to the Red Army. Following recuperation from his injuries he was sent back to the Eastern Front in the spring of 1943 where he commanded the LXXXII Army Corps. From June 25 he was given the command of the Seventeenth Army defending positions in southern Russia.

As a commander Jaenecke was intelligent, shrewd, and had a high moral code of safeguarding his men on the battlefield, despite his loyalty to Hitler. As a tactician he was a master of defense and led his men to safety through a series of tactical withdrawals that ultimately saved the lives of many soldiers. Unlike other commanders in the field, he was not a brutal commander but was an efficient and effective leader. Despite his tendency to constantly request permission to withdraw to save his lines from annihilation, Hitler relied on his nerve to hold the front in the Crimea.

On April 29 the general flew to Berchtesgaden where he met Hitler to discuss the dire situation in the Crimea. Jaenecke's insistence that Sevastopol be evacuated because his army, now cut off, should be withdrawn to save the lives of some 235,000 men incensed Hitler, who ordered him to hold Sevastopol as a fortress, as the Soviets had done during the first Crimean campaign in 1941–42. However, thousands of troops were already being withdrawn from the peninsula by sea under the codename Operation *60,000*, and it was too late to avert the evacuation. Hitler was enraged and accused Jaenecke of treason. He was relieved of his command forthwith and blamed for the loss of the Crimea. He was later arrested in Romania and subsequently court-martialed. A report was filed against him with General Heinz Guderian appointed as a special investigator, but Jaenecke was acquitted in June 1944. He was dismissed from the army on January 31, 1945. Six months later Jaenecke was arrested by the Soviet authorities for crimes committed under his command in 1942 and was sentenced to 25 years' hard labor. He was released in 1955.

While areas in the north of the peninsula were being strengthened, in the south the old Russian fortifications—destroyed during the siege of Sevastopol in 1941—were quickly repaired. Fortunately for the Germans, although cut off from the mainland by the 4th Ukrainian Front, the peninsula was still being supplied from the port of Odessa and the Romanian port of Constanta. The Luftwaffe too was able to bring reinforcements and evacuate the wounded. For the time being the Germans still held on to the Crimea.

During early 1944 the German Seventeenth Army was almost left in peace. However, there was a pending sense of futility and gloom, as the situation on the Eastern Front worsened, especially in the south. Yet as German divisions on the mainland were being destroyed, infantry divisions on the peninsula had little to do other than build defenses, perform guard duties, and undertake endless reconnaissance missions. Only the Luftwaffe and Kriegsmarine were busy, bringing in supplies and keeping the Soviet Black Sea Fleet at bay.

Since the summer of 1943 the German Army had been steadily retreating across Russia. Its withdrawal was not just because of overwhelming Red Army forces but because of intelligence failures, defensive doctrines, and loss of air superiority. By the spring of 1944, the situation on the Eastern Front, especially in the Ukraine and in the Crimea, marked a significant turning point. German military intelligence had failed numerous times to determine the main direction of the Soviet advance, and as a result its defensive doctrine was often disastrous. German forces also had limited mobile infantry reserves to hold positions for any length of time. Reserves, notably its scarce panzer divisions, were now being used to prevent encirclement. Hitler's defensive policy of "standing fast" was another reason that the German Army struggled to defend. He forbade any type of flexible defense that could allow the Wehrmacht time to withdraw and counterattack to meet growing Soviet attacks. Instead, German forces often had to fight for their very survival in breaking out to the rear. Because of the speed of the enemy and the need for the German soldier to escape annihilation, vital weaponry and equipment were regularly discarded. As Soviet forces pushed farther west across the Dnieper River and south into the Crimean Peninsula, Hitler established by decree various fortresses to halt the Soviet drive. However, his rigid defense policy did not work for any length of time given the overwhelming might of Soviet firepower and its mobility on the battlefield. By tying down German forces and turning cities and ports into fortresses, he consequently deprived his commanders of any flexibility in deploying reserves to counter the enemy. This type of defensive strategy ultimately saw the front being vastly overextended and resulted in massive material and personnel losses.

Another contribution to the inability of the German Army to defend its positions was its loss of air superiority. In fact, even in the summer of 1941 the Luftwaffe had been overextended despite its successes. This situation only worsened as the spring of 1944 approached. In the Crimea, the Luftwaffe was totally overstretched and unable to wage any type of strategic warfare, being forced into a defensive role.

Yet, despite these failures by the German Army and its Luftwaffe, the German defensive policy in southern Ukraine was not unsuccessful. German commanders, especially in the Crimea, managed to coordinate their artillery against numerous Soviet attacks. Soviet strategic and tactical errors also helped. In short, the Red Army had diverted its attention

In Profile:
General Fyodor Tolbukhin

Born into a peasant family, Tolbukhin volunteered for the Imperial Russian Army during World War I where he served with distinction and was promoted captain. Decorated for his actions in the field, he later served as the chief of staff of the 56th Infantry Division and during the 1930s took several staff positions. It was not until August 1941 during the German invasion of Russia that he was made chief of staff of the Crimean Front, and then assistant commander of the Stalingrad Military District in 1942. It was in this position that Tolbukhin excelled as a leader. He was ruthless and effective on the battlefield, which Stalin admired. At Stalingrad he commanded the 57th Army where he was praised for his strategy in trapping the enemy and destroying him. Following the victorious capture of Stalingrad, he was placed in command of the Southern Front, which in October 1943 was renamed 4th Ukrainian Front. Once again, he demonstrated his leadership. Being strong-willed, tough, decisive, and ruthless on the battlefield, he led his front along with the 3rd Ukrainian Front in the Lower Dnieper Offensive and the Dnieper–Carpathian Offensive. It was his troops, the 2nd Guards and 51st Armies, who forced the German Seventeenth Army to withdraw into the Crimean Peninsula. The Germans were unable to prevent Tolbukhin's advance that reached Kerch and then Simferopol. The general's plan was to squeeze the German Seventeenth Army and its Axis troops toward Sevastopol where he knew they would either evacuate by sea or be slowly reduced inside the old fortifications. As a commander he was careful and precise, and his tactical brilliance saw him force the enemy out of the Crimea. Following this success Tolbukhin took over the 3rd Ukrainian Front and launched the Red Army summer campaign to capture the Balkans, between June and October 1944.

temporarily from the Crimea as they knew that German forces on the peninsula had nowhere to escape, except by sea. But unbeknown to the Germans the Soviets in early 1944 were already undertaking careful procedures in southern Ukraine to conceal offensive preparations against the Crimea. The winter was another contribution in delaying the Soviet offensive, and allowed the Germans more time to build additional defenses and strengthen the port of Sevastopol. However, as with most other areas being held on the Eastern Front, Hitler's refusal to develop more defensive positions in depth meant that when the enemy attacked in strength there were no proper defensive lines in the rear on which the German troops could fall back.

One of the most important areas of defense during the winter of 1943/44 was the Perekop Isthmus and the easternmost tip of the Kerch Peninsula. Hitler, with his *Festungen* policy, had outlined the importance of holding these positions and told his commanders that the loss of the Perekop Isthmus would mean that only Sevastopol could make a stand. To prevent such a loss, troops had built what was known as the Gneisenau Line, a staggered line of defenses around Simferopol to defend Sevastopol. In fact, General Schörner who inspected the Crimea defenses pronounced on April 7, 1944, that the "peninsula could be held for a long time." He couldn't have been more wrong.

By 1943 the Red Army had entered a decisive phase in its strategy against the German Army. Soviet troops were now using surprise, maneuver, and overwhelming firepower to destroy the enemy. They also used their tank armies to full effect, where its formations supported by massed infantry achieved numerous breakthroughs. These tactics were particularly effective in southern Russia and in the Ukraine, achieved by wearing down the enemy first to gain ground. The objective was to destroy the enemy, but it was important to attack in weight to accomplish the fatal blow. As a result, especially in the Ukraine, the Red Army transitioned from defensive to offensive operations. However, the Soviets were not equipped for rapid advances over long distances, but the Red Army soldier was a master of survival and was expected to survive through forage and battlefield booty wherever possible.

By the early winter of 1943/44 as the Eastern Front stagnated in the snow, the Red Army had advanced hundreds of miles. They had secured bridgeheads across the Dnieper River and isolated the German Seventeenth Army in the Crimea. In the air the Soviet Air Force dominated the skies and was employed en masse to overwhelm enemy ground and flak positions.

Another factor of Soviet success was Lend-Lease, which contributed greatly toward the collapse of the German Army in Russia. By the end of 1943 Allied shipments to Russia totaled 173,000 vehicles and 4,300 tanks. During the last year of the war almost 11.1 million tons of Lend-Lease supplies were sent to the Eastern Front.

In short, by 1944 Stalin had reversed the early setbacks of his army on the Eastern Front. His strategy to defeat the enemy was to maintain overwhelming firepower and mobility. Manpower and material combined ensured a formidable land army. The main thrust of the ground forces centered on using massed tank and motorized divisions to achieve surprise whenever possible and to strive to continuously seize and hold the initiative. Even during the dark days when the Germans first launched *Barbarossa*, the Soviet leadership maintained its strategy to exert itself at great expense in men and material to achieve its objectives and expel the invaders from the "Motherland."

In Profile: Rear Admiral Horia Macellariu

When Romania entered the war and allied itself with Germany against the Soviet Union, Horia Macellariu was appointed chief of staff of the Romanian Navy on the Romanian General Staff. As the war progressed, in January 1942 he became commander of the powerful Romanian Squadron in the Black Sea. By March 1943 he was promoted commander of the Romanian Black Sea Fleet with the rank of rear admiral. As admiral of the fleet, he had significant power over all Axis shipping in the Black Sea and was effectively one of the most important commanders in southern Russia. It was here he significantly enlarged the Romanian Black Sea Fleet where he commissioned Romanian-built submarines for operations against the Soviets. He also commissioned Italian vessels too, including midget submarines. As a commander, he was influential, efficient, effective, and believed the Axis would win the war against the Soviets. However, by 1944, with Axis forces withdrawing across Russia, Ukraine, and into the Crimea, Macellariu began planning with General Jaenecke, commander of the German Seventeenth Army, to evacuate thousands of troops in what would become the most difficult and elaborate operation of the Romanian Navy. Various German and Romanian warships would escort convoys between Constanta and Sevastopol using all four Romanian destroyers in the Black Sea. Despite being under constant Red Army aerial and ground bombardment, the Axis ships under Macellariu's leadership saw some 30,000 soldiers transported in four days during the last phase of the evacuation operation. In total, between mid-April and May 1944 some 113,000 Axis troops were evacuated from the Crimea. Despite Hitler's reluctance in allowing Axis forces to evacuate the Crimea, thanks to General Jaenecke, he respected Macellariu's achievements. As a result, the admiral was bestowed the Knight's Cross of the Iron Cross and decorated with the Order of the Star of Romania and the Order of the German Eagle including the Order of Michael the Brave. However, weeks later, with Romania switching sides, German Vice Admiral Helmuth Brinkmann was ordered to hold Constanta to the last man. Yet, despite this order, following a meeting with Macellariu, the German admiral was persuaded to retreat to avoid complete annihilation by the Red Army. Brinkmann subsequently began withdrawing his forces from Constanta during the night of August 25/26. The withdrawal saw the admiral later receiving Soviet forces in Constanta, and the takeover by the British Royal Navy on September 5, 1944.

In Profile:
Wehrmacht Defense of the Crimea

MG 42 Machine Gunners, Gneisenau Line, the Crimea, April 11, 1944

Along the Gneisenau Line on the Crimea German and Romanian troops set up MG 42 machine-gun positions. This defensive line, in a large semi-circle centered on Sevastopol, from Evpatoriya on the west coast to Alushta on the south coast, included Simferopol and Yalta. This weapon, mounted on a Lafette 42 tripod, was highly reliable and simple to operate. It had a high rate of fire of 1,200 rounds per minute. (Renato Dalmaso)

German Nashorn Geschützwagen III/IV (Sd. Kfz. 164) Tanker, the Crimea, April 1944

From an unidentified Panzerjäger battalion, this smiling tanker eats a slice of bread. He wears the German Army reversible green splinter-pattern jacket. The reversible uniform was designed so that it was large enough to be worn over the service uniform, including personal equipment. (Renato Dalmaso)

German Order of Battle, February 2, 1944

Seventeenth Army

V Army Corps

- 73rd German Infantry Division
- 98th German Infantry Division
- 3rd Romanian Mountain Division
- 6th Romanian Cavalry Division

XXXXIX Mountain Corps

- Group Conrad
- 50th German Infantry Division
- 336th German Infantry Division
- 9th Romanian Cavalry Division

Romanian Cavalry Corps

- 10th Infantry Division
- 19th Infantry Division

1st Romanian Mountain Corps

- Fortress Commander Sevastopol
- 1st Mountain Division
- 2nd Mountain Division

Reserves

- 111th Infantry Division

Source: Wikipedia

In Profile:
General Georgiy Fedorovich Zakharov

During the early months of the German invasion of the Soviet Union Zakharov served as chief of staff of the 22nd Army. He quickly demonstrated his leadership qualities. Stalin saw him as a man that would never say no and who stubbornly ignored reports of the German troop movements. Although Zakharov was totally aware initially that the Red Army was unable to stop the German war machine, he was perceptive enough to see that a flexible mobile defense was key to retaining ground and successfully counterattacking. Zakharov's tactics and toughness saw him in November 1941 become commander of the Bryansk Front, and a month later deputy commander of the Western Front, responsible for employing blocking formations in front of Moscow. From April 1942 he became chief of staff of the North Caucasian Strategic Direction and then the North Caucasian Front. Later that year, he became deputy commander of the Stalingrad Front where his exceptional leadership skills saw the Red Army counterattack. In January 1943 he was promoted commander of the Southern Front, and then a few weeks later the 51st Army. From July 1943 he was given the command of the 2nd Guards Army and led his formations against retreating German forces in southern Russia and Ukraine. By April 1944 his powerful units had smashed through the German fortified positions on the Perekop Isthmus in preparation for the liberation of Sevastopol.

Soviet Order of Battle, April 1944

4th Ukrainian Front

Units subordinated to the Front

- 35th Tank-destroyer Artillery Brigade, 530th Tank-Destroyer Artillery Regiment, 4th Guards Mortar Brigade (13th, 30th, 31st Guards Mortar Regiment), 2nd, 4th, 19th, 21st, 23rd, 67th Guards Mortar Regiments, 270th Guards AA Artillery Regiment (from 18th Anti-Aircraft Artillery Division), 1069th AA Artillery Regiment (from 2nd Division), 1485th Anti-Aircraft Artillery Regiment
- 19th Tank Corps (79th, 101st, 202nd Tank Brigades, 26th Motorized Rifle Brigade, 867th, 875th SP Artillery Regiments, 91st Motorcycle Battalion, 1511th Tank-Destroyer Artillery Regiment, 179th Mortar Regiment, 1717th AA Artillery Regiment)
    - 6th Guards Tank Brigade, 52nd Motorcycle Regiment, 5th Separate Armored Car Battalion, 46th and 54th Separate Armored Train Battalions
- 7th Engineer-Sapper Brigade, 2nd Pontoon-Bridge Brigade, 3rd Guards, 65th, 240th Separate Engineer Battalions, 17th Guards Mine Battalion, 102nd Pontoon-Bridge Battalion (from 5th Pontoon-Bridge Brigade)

2nd Guards Army

- 13th Guards Rifle Corps
    - 3rd Guards Rifle Division
    - 24th Guards Rifle Division
    - 87th Guards Rifle Division
- 54th Rifle Corps
    - 126th Rifle Division
    - 315th Rifle Division
    - 387th Rifle Division

- 55th Rifle Corps
  - 87th Rifle Division
  - 347th Rifle Division
  - 116th Fortified Region
  - 2nd Guards Breakthrough Artillery Division (4th Guards Light Artillery Brigade, 114 Gun Artillery Brigade, 5th Guards Howitzer Artillery Brigade, 20th Guards High Power Howitzer Artillery Brigade, 33rd Mortar Brigade)
- Independent (Army) units: 1095th, 1101st Gun Artillery Regiments, 331st Howitzer Artillery Regiment, 315th and 317th Artillery Battalions of High Impact (heavy artillery), 113th Guards, 14th 1250th Tank-Destroyer Artillery Regiments, 133rd Guards, 483rd Mortar Regiments (MRL), 76th AA Artillery Division (223rd, 416th, 447th AA Artillery Regiments), 591st, 1530th AA Artillery Regiments
- 1452nd SP Artillery Regiment, 512 Independent Tank Battalion
- 43rd Special Purpose Engineer Brigade, Independent 258th and 255th Engineer Battalions

51st Army

- 1st Guards Rifle Corps (33rd Guards, 91st, 346th RD)
- 10th Rifle Corps (216th, 357th, 279th Rifle Divisions)
- 63rd Rifle Corps (263rd, 267th, 417th Rifle Divisions)
  - 77th Rifle Division
  - 78th Fortified Region
  - 26th Artillery Division (75th Light Artillery Brigade, 56th Gun Artillery Brigade, 77th Howitzer Brigade)
- Independent (Army) units: 6th Guards Gun Artillery Brigade (from 2nd Guards Breakthrough Artillery Division), 105th High Impact Howitzer Artillery Brigade (from 7th Breakthrough Artillery Division), 647th, 1105th Gun Artillery Regiments, 85th Guards, 1231st Howitzer Artillery Regiment,

207th Guards Howitzer Artillery Regiment (from 5th Guards Howitzer Artillery Brigade), 5th Guards, 15th, 21st Tank-destroyer Artillery Brigades, 764th 1246th Tank-destroyer Artillery Regiment, 19th Mortar Brigade, 125th Mortar Regiment.

- Anti-Aircraft Artillery forces
    - 2nd Anti-Aircraft Artillery Division (1086th, 1113th, 1117th AA Artillery Regiment)
    - 15th Anti-Aircraft Artillery Division (281st, 342nd, 723rd, 1264th AA Artillery Regiments)
    - 18th Anti-Aircraft Artillery Division (160th and 166th Guards, 297th AA Artillery Regiments) 77th Guards Artillery Regiment
    - 32nd Guards Tank Brigade, 22nd Guards Separate Tank Regiment, 30th and 33rd Separate Armored Train Battalions
    - 12th Assault Engineer Brigade, 63rd Engineer-Sapper Brigade, 5th Guards, 1504 Separate Engineer Battalions, 275th Separate Sapper Battalion

Source: Wikipedia

In Profile:
Soviet Tanks

Soviet IS-2 Tank, 6th Guards Tank Brigade, 4th Ukrainian Front, Parpach Line, April 12, 1944

This Red Army heavy tank—IS standing for Joseph Stalin—was usually supplied to the elite Guards heavy tank regiments. In the Crimea these tanks were reserved for crucial attacks, often to spearhead attempts to break through fortified German positions like antitank defensive lines and bunkers. The tank is painted in overall olive green for summer operations. (Oliver Missing)

Soviet T-34-85 Tank, 6th Guards Tank Brigade, 4th Ukrainian Front, Bakhchysarai, April 15, 1944

This Soviet medium tank painted in its summer camouflage scheme of olive green had better armor and mobility than the German Pz.Kpfw. IV panzer and Sturmgeschütz III assault gun. It was used with great success against German defenses in the Crimea. (Oliver Missing)

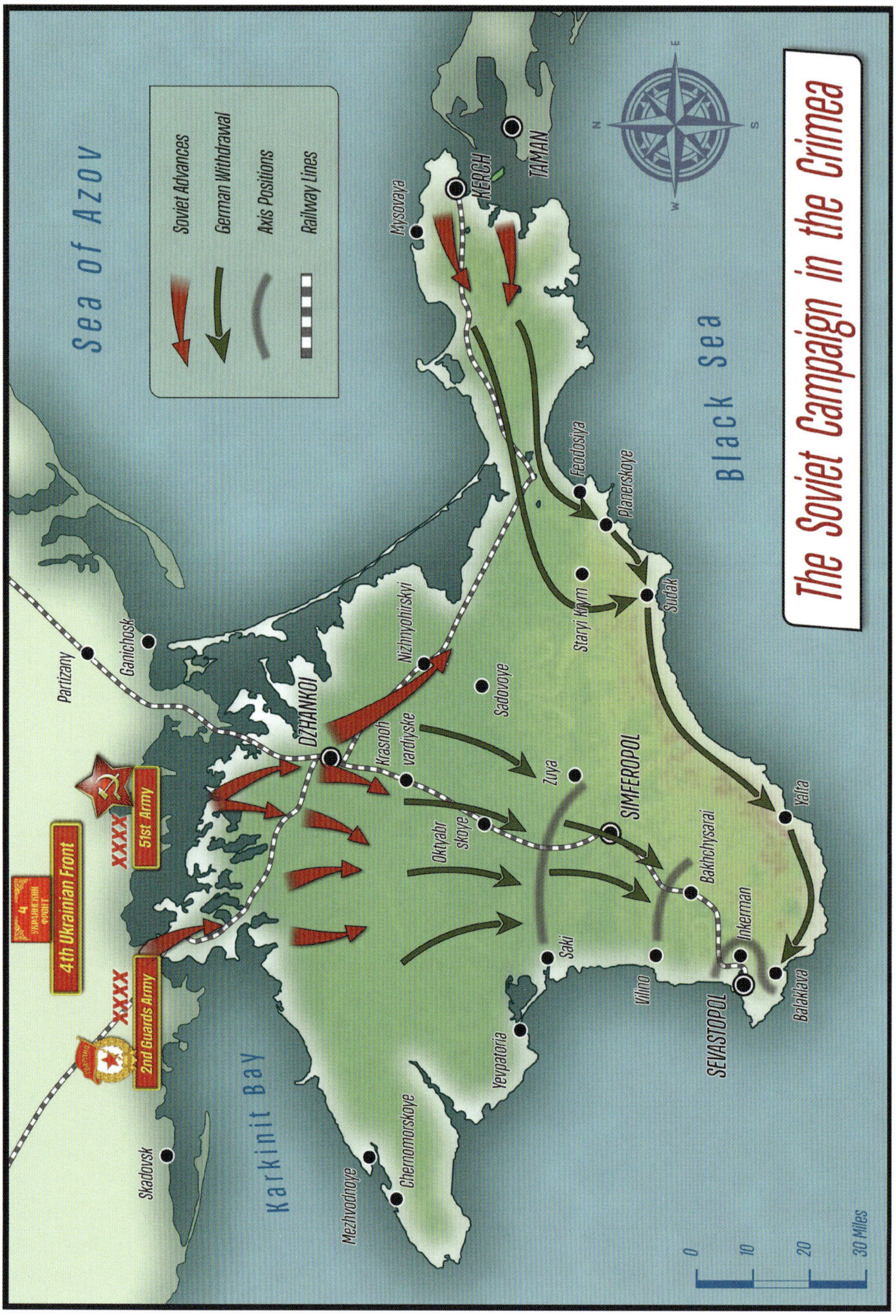

Russian forces advance southwards onto the peninsula towards Sevastopol. (Anderson Subtil)

The Crimean Offensive, April 8–May 12, 1944

Following the Soviet Kerch–Eltigen Operation in late 1943, by March 1944 Stavka decided it was time to divert some of its forces to the Crimea, capture the peninsula, and liberate Sevastopol. In the weeks preceding, plans for the Crimean offensive in southern Ukraine had been hampered by melting snow followed by heavy rains. Roads were turned into quagmires, rivers flooded, and terrain proved almost impossible for mechanized units to maneuver. However, by mid-March the weather had improved, and Stavka began formulating an attack into the Crimea. Strung out along southern Ukraine were various Red Army units and formations all preparing to move forward at a moment's notice. Careful procedures were especially utilized along the southern sector of the front to conceal the offensive preparations between Skadovs'k in the west and Heniches'k in the east. Along this sector of the front was the 4th Ukrainian Front that had been given the task of liberating the peninsula.

A Soviet mortar battery in action.

It was perceived that the remaining Axis forces would then be forced to fight for their survival in a major breakout to the rear and in the process discard whatever heavy equipment they had left. Remnants of the German Army would then support troops defending Sevastopol. Stavka assumed that Hitler would use the port, as the Soviets had done in 1941 and 1942, by turning it into a fortress. This strategy was merely to prolong and tie down Red Army forces on the peninsula, hoping that it would hinder further operations for the other Ukrainian fronts fighting west of the Dnieper. Soviet intelligence monitored increased enemy shipping in the Black Sea, which it deduced might be used to evacuate troops from Sevastopol to Constanta. As a result, the Black Sea Fleet, which was subordinated to the Southern Military District of the Soviet Armed Forces, was put on alert. However, the Soviet surface fleet was practically non-operational. So, smaller vessels and the small Soviet Naval Air Force were made operational from the port of Odessa that was liberated in March 1944.

By November 1943, the Red Army had secured the beachheads on the southern shore of the Sivash and on the Kerch Peninsula, ensuring that General Jaenecke's Seventeenth Army was trapped in the Crimea. While his forces constructed defenses to hold back the enemy, Jaenecke reasoned that the peninsula could not be held for any appreciable length of time. Hitler, however, was determined to hold the Crimea and promised that the Seventeenth Army would be increased in strength. By early 1944 the main defensive line on the Perekop Isthmus had managed to reduce the Red Army beachheads to two small parcels of land, one at the southeastern end of the Kerch Peninsula. It was planned that when the Soviets launched their attack and the Perekop Isthmus was captured, Jaenecke would task his Seventeenth Army to make a stand at Sevastopol.

A Soviet 82mm mortar crew attached to the 4th Ukrainian Front's 2nd Guards sets up on high ground, April 1944.

In Profile:
General Yakov Grigorevich Kreizer

Before the German invasion of the Soviet Union in June 1941, Kreizer was commander of the 1st Moscow Motorized Rifle Division. When the Germans attacked, he was among the few commanders in the field who had prepared his positions to block the enemy advance. As a commander he believed in organizing effective defense, instilling draconian discipline, and repairing morale. He told his men that there would be no retreat and that he would counterattack wherever and whenever possible. Unyielding in the face of his adversary, his men outfought the Wehrmacht in one large battle in the summer of 1941, but despite the brave counterattack, the Germans were far superior; however, Kreizer made a skillful withdrawal causing significant enemy casualties. His achievements saw him promoted major general in the 3rd Army, with Stalin bestowing on him Hero of the Soviet Union. Under his command the 3rd Army managed to slow the German advance and was an integral part in the strategic end to the German blitzkrieg campaign in Russia. During the battle of Stalingrad Kreizer was made deputy commander of the 2nd Guards Army. Once again, he showed how creative and innovative he could be in defense as well as in attack. He was regarded as an all-round commander, but above all a master tactician. In August 1943 he was promoted to command the 51st Army that played a decisive role in defeating Axis forces in the Ukraine and the Crimea.

One of the thousands of German foxholes dug along the front in the Crimea.

German and Romanian officers survey the terrain.

Soviet troops advance in the Crimea, past a knocked-out German Sturmgeschütz III.

A Soviet 82mm mortar crew rush across a field during an advance.

A Red Army 120mm mortar crew. This weapon saw extensive service during the war and hurled a monstrous 16kg shell. The soldier priming the shells in front has his head bandaged.

Early on the morning of April 8, 1944, the 4th Ukrainian Front began moving long columns of vehicles, guns, and men forward to their assembly areas. Under trees, beside the roads, hundreds of antitank and antiaircraft guns of all calibers were moved in preparation for supporting the infantry. Katyusha rocket launchers and artillery pieces had already been positioned and concealed under camouflage netting for mile upon mile. Tanks and self-propelled guns began moving forward and behind them assault detachments and advanced battalions followed closely. As these Red Army units prepared to attack, the morning quiet was broken by shouts from Soviet gunnery officers giving the order for the artillery batteries to begin the preliminary barrage. The bombardment was to soften the German defenses and allow company- and battalion-sized infantry units to attack. Along the entire Soviet front, the whole area erupted in a wall of flame and smoke as artillery and Katyusha multiple rocket launchers poured fire onto the German defenses, which were immediately engulfed in huge explosions.

The initial offensive saw Soviet artillery supporting reconnaissance attacks, pulverizing positions, and destroying areas deep into the German lines. Soviet artillery pounded enemy trenches and fortifications along the Isthmus Line for almost an hour, and then the infantry and armor were ordered to attack. When the artillery barrage lifted, much of the German front had held despite overwhelming odds. The first major Soviet assault deployed troops and armor across the Perekop Isthmus using elements of the 4th Ukrainian Front's 2nd Guards and 51st Armies. For hours German and Romanian defenses endured relentless fire.

A T-34 advancing across a field supported by Soviet fighter aircraft.

German soldiers navigate a flooded trench following a downpour.

The Romanian 10th Division bore the brunt but managed to cling on to the line of the Sivash bridgehead. However, inevitably, due to overwhelming enemy firepower these Axis forces would soon be reduced and the remnants withdrawn southward toward Sevastopol.

During the afternoon the Soviet offensive continued along the entire front. German intelligence was overwhelmed. The speed and depth of the offensive saw the German and Romanian front begin to buckle. Along parts of the front German units were simply brushed aside, and those forbidden from retreating were annihilated. In the mayhem and confusion that engulfed the German defenses, General Schörner held an urgent war conference and told General Kurt Zeitzler, chief of the General Staff of the German high command, that a reluctant retreat to Sevastopol might have to begin any minute. They agreed that orders were to be sent to the Crimea for Jaenecke to authorize a major withdrawal of the Seventeenth Army. Hitler, however, blatantly refused. Instead, he dispatched Zeitzler to army group headquarters to prevent a rout. When Zeitzler arrived on April 10, he was told that the Red Army had already driven its spearheads into the interior of the Crimea and that the first stage of the German retreat had begun in earnest. Reports confirmed that German and Romanian forces had withdrawn from the Kerch Peninsula southeastward to prevent annihilation. Hitler had initially approved this withdrawal, but then learned that Seventeenth Army formations had also prematurely withdrawn to the Gneisenau Line. The whole front was collapsing, and Hitler blamed its leadership for the disarray. He was particularly scathing of Jaenecke and fell into a rage accusing the general of losing his nerve.

A Soviet mortar crew is moving to another position during intense fighting.

A Soviet machine gunner and his number two manning a captured German MG 34.

A Soviet soldier shaves in a captured German trench. In the foreground are a PPSh-41 submachine gun and a high-explosive RG-42 grenade.

Romanian troops in the Crimea, April 1944.

A Red Army ISU-152 advances across a field.

A wounded Soviet soldier is carried to a field dressing station by a comrade.

Red Army troops escort a captured German soldier back to the rear following intense fighting in Kerch. The German has been lightly wounded in his right arm or hand.

Out on the front lines German field commanders continued trying to hold their men together against overwhelming enemy superiority. However, the lines could not be held and as the Germans retreated west of the Kerch, the Independent Coastal Army launched a series of assaults from the east. This army had two corps, the 11th Guards Rifle Corps and 16th Guards Rifle Corps, totaling 12 rifle divisions, two rifle brigades, and one independent tank brigade supported by 212 tanks and 961 artillery pieces.

The Soviets were facing General Karl Allmendinger's V Army Corps comprised of the 73rd and 98th Infantry Divisions, 6th Romanian Cavalry, and 3rd Romanian Mountain Divisions. The situation for this German army corps looked perilous and Allmendinger sent

Soviet troops in fine spirits march to the front.

A German antitank gun crew wait for the enemy.

A Soviet 82mm mortar crew prepare their weapon for action.

A Soviet T-34-85 in a field supported by a 45mm antitank gun.

A T-34-85 fords a river on the way to Sevastopol.

A fine photograph of a column of T-34-85 tanks with motorcycle combinations.

A T-34 tank with infantry hitching a ride moving into action in muddy terrain.

a frantic message appealing to Jaenecke that his forces were unable to hold their positions for much longer. Luckily for him, both Schörner and the Army Group South Ukraine chief of staff were in the Crimea and could see for themselves the unfolding catastrophe. They both agreed that Jaenecke's decision to withdraw his troops to the Gneisenau Line was necessary to prevent annihilation. As a result, Hitler relented and ordered the Seventeenth Army's withdrawal. If necessary, he said, soldiers would have to be withdrawn to Sevastopol but made it clear to his commanders that the port must be held at all costs, and indefinitely. Schörner countered and made it clear to Hitler that both the Gneisenau Line and Sevastopol

Very young disheveled and exhausted German POWs.

Soviet troops charge across open terrain toward the German lines.

could not be held for more than three or four weeks. For that reason, he said, the last stage of the operation would mean an evacuation from the Crimea. In anticipation of such, he had already ordered the navy to send a convoy of ships from Constanta, Romania, to remove all service troops.

Soviet troops of the Coastal Army in action. It was this army that first defeated the rearguard of German forces north of Kerch.

In Profile:
Soviet AA Artillery and M1943 Mortar Troops

Soviet 85mm M1939 (52-K) Gunners, 1485th Anti-Aircraft Artillery Regiment, 4th Ukrainian Front, Ternivka, April 15, 1944

A Soviet air defense battery set up outside Sevastopol near the town of Ternivka. These guns were organized into heavy antiaircraft regiments of 16 guns. (Renato Dalmaso)

M1943 Mortar (120-PM-43) Troops, 67th Guards Mortar Regiment, 4th Ukrainian Front, Sevastopol, late April 1944

Red Army mortar crews go into action around Sevastopol. These large 120mm mortars were so impressive on the battlefield that the Germans copied the design. (Renato Dalmaso)

Following Hitler's retreat order, Allmendinger received the "*Adler*" (Eagle) message to withdraw his army corps. What followed was a 150-mile race to the Gneisenau Line, with the Soviet Independent Coastal Army in hot pursuit. The vanguard of the V Corps retreat saw German units pull back to what was known as the Parpach Line that stretched across the narrowest part of the Kerch Peninsula. Despite suffering huge losses and leaving behind some armor and guns to escape the clutches of the Red Army advance, the German divisions still retaliated and knocked out several enemy tanks. In fact, the Germans were able to employ artillery as a main line of defense and stall the Soviet advance in several places. However, the Parpach Line could not be held. Allmendinger was concerned by the large Soviet formations moving from the north and threatening the rear of his V Corps. As a result, he ordered the Parpach positions to be abandoned and his troops to make for the Gneisenau Line. Several units had placed themselves in the mountain passes and main crossroads, setting up strategically placed antitank positions. However, the Yalta Mountains proved challenging for the horses towing larger-caliber guns. As a result, Allmendinger ordered that the artillery be destroyed. Although this allowed the infantry to move faster, it deprived him of vital artillery support. When V Corps arrived at the Gneisenau Line, the Soviets were already attacking it.

Elsewhere in the Crimea the situation for the Germans further deteriorated as they frantically contested each position. On April 11 the Soviet Separate Coastal Army reached Simferopol, 37 miles northeast of Sevastopol. The following day the Gneisenau Line was torn open in several places by Soviet tanks. German and Romanian forces quickly found themselves overwhelmed, bombarded into submission. In several places they found that the speed of the Red Army advance meant that they were unable to mount any type of resistance. In the chaos and disorder that ensued hundreds of disheartened and frightened soldiers fled their foxholes and fortifications to avoid annihilation.

A staged photo of a Soviet attack using a smokescreen to conceal the infantry charge. These types of attack were common in the Red Army.

Pack animals belonging to the Soviet 3rd Mountain Rifle Corps transporting ammunition to the front on the Kerch Peninsula.

Along part of the captured coastline showing destroyed German vehicles.

Red Army infantry and coastal troops storm a German defensive position on the Sevastopol shoreline.

As for the Red Army, their tactics were unchanged: to attack on a broad front by concentrating large numbers of infantry supported by heavy artillery and armor. The Germans were already experiencing various defensive issues and despite some of the stronger defenses, which were often manned with antitank guns and lines of machine-gun pits, Soviet infantry charged in their hundreds regardless of the cost in life to their own ranks. As a result, large areas of the Crimea were taken. Simferopol, the second largest town and the main defensive position for the Germans north of Sevastopol, was captured on April 12. This allowed Soviet mechanized units to pour onto the main highway south and capture Chisten'koye and Pohtovoye. Leading elements then drove at breakneck speed toward the town of Bakhchysarai but were halted by German defenses.

By April 15 the Seventeenth Army was under considerable pressure and being pushed to fight a rearguard action on the main Sevastopol line. Fighting continued to rage outside Sevastopol with unabated ferocity with the bulk of German and Romanian forces retreating toward the port by April 16. Hitler once again communicated to Jaenecke, instructing him that Sevastopol was to be held at all costs. However, despite this "Führer Order," Hitler knew that the Crimea was already lost. A day later he instructed Army Group South Ukraine to divest itself of all infantry and equipment not required for the defense of the peninsula, and to hold Sevastopol as a fortress for as long as possible. Simultaneously, evacuation by sea was being prepared to transport troops to Constanta.

On April 16 German forces began withdrawing into the main Sevastopol line to take up defenses there. Intermingled with the withdrawing soldiers were the wounded too. Within 10 days of the Soviet offensive into the Crimea there were an estimated 13,000 German and 18,000 Romanian casualties. Ration strength of the Seventeenth Army was 75,546 Germans and 45,887 Romanians. However, the Romanian troops were reported to be in bad shape and not fit for combat, and it was deemed by the German high command that they should be evacuated from Sevastopol.

In total the Germans and Axis forces had five *Kampfgruppen* each of roughly regimental strength facing three massive Soviet armies with a total strength of 27 divisions and 200 tanks. Jaenecke knew that Sevastopol could not be held because his army lacked strength, and the navy could not keep pace with the amount of supplies required to keep his army fighting. He reported to Schörner that his force was severely battered, supported only by a motley collection of assault guns, artillery, and antiaircraft guns that had survived the retreat. Allmendinger told Jaenecke that his V Corps was severely understrength and could not hold out. His corps had joined Rudolf Konrad's XXXXIX Mountain Corps on April 16 and was employed along the northern line surrounding Sevastopol. Allmendinger had lost most of his heavy artillery and had hundreds of wounded soldiers incapable of withstanding any kind of attack.

As for the Soviet armies bearing down on Sevastopol, it was only a matter of time before they broke through into the city. For several days, Soviet artillery pounded the port and the German defensive lines. From the town of Simferopol on the main road to Sevastopol Soviet armor and infantry columns advanced south. Often, they were halted by German resistance that had set up defensive positions in the foothills of the Crimean Mountains. But despite this opposition, the Soviets broke through with overwhelming strength.

Soviet troops fire their weapons in the air in celebration at the bay in Sevastopol. Damaged transports litter the bay.

Red Army coastal troops in Sevastopol. These troops were reassigned to the 4th Ukrainian Front on April 18.

To avert annihilation of the Seventeenth Army an emergency war conference was held on April 21 in an atmosphere reminiscent of the problems the Germans had faced at Stalingrad. During the meeting Hitler told Jaenecke that he was a "defeatist," and his men could hold Sevastopol. All he needed, Hitler said, was reinforcements and his troops would be able to hold out for six to eight weeks. However, Jaenecke rebuked Hitler's "unrealistic" assessment of the situation and told him that he needed to order an evacuation. Hitler refused to believe that the Seventeenth Army could not hold out, so fighting continued unabated around Sevastopol.

Sailors of the Black Sea Fleet raise the Soviet flag over Sevastopol.

Jaenecke continued to call for the evacuation of his troops before it was too late. His men were holding several positions at great cost, but he reported that some areas were being lost due to growing Soviet superiority. On April 28, the general was ordered to Berchtesgaden where Hitler once again told him he would receive more reinforcements. To Jaenecke's surprise, the reinforcements amounted to only four battalions of poorly trained men. There was another argument and Hitler then told the general that he had lost his nerve and was not up to the job to conduct a proper defense. He was replaced by Allmendinger. Although Allmendinger was a capable commander, he too was unable to avert the inevitable onslaught of the Red Army. The Soviets continued remorselessly to advance and fight their way down to Sevastopol.

Despite the changes in command nothing could avert the dire situation of the Seventeenth Army. By early May the Red Army's Independent Coastal Army was placed under the direct command of Tolbukhin, who now had 470,000 troops, 600 tanks, and 6,000 guns and mortars at his disposal, all poised to assault Sevastopol. Tolbukhin planned for a two-pronged assault using his 2nd Guards Army against the northern defenses of Sevastopol. The 51st Army would support the Independent Coastal Army and open the main attack from the east and southeast.

At 9:30 am on May 5, Red Army artillery positions opened a massive bombardment with some 300 guns and mortars, pulverizing the German front. Simultaneously, while the German positions were being decimated, the 2nd Guards Army launched a series of attacks in the north and Kreizer's 51st Army attacked the Sapun Hills. Fighting along the German front was fierce and unrelenting. The Soviet 63rd Rifle Corps spearheaded the main attack

A sailor belonging to the Black Sea Fleet raises the Soviet flag over Sevastopol.

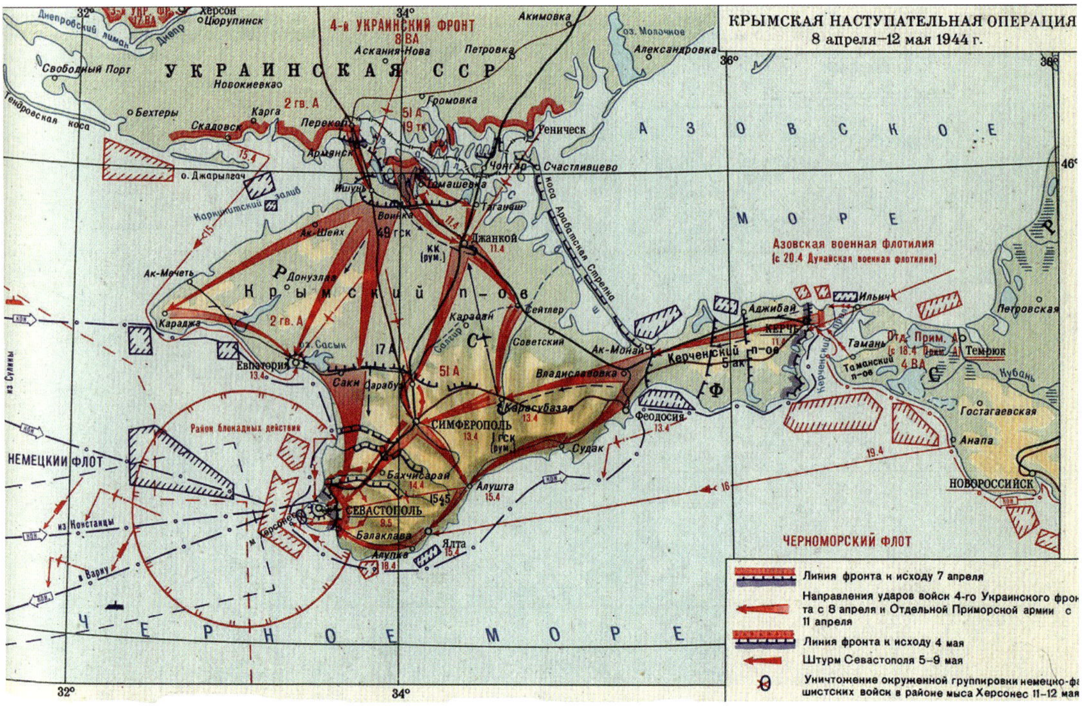

A Soviet map showing the disposition and advance of Soviet forces across the Crimea and surrounding Sevastopol in April/May 1944.
(By Mil.ru, CC BY 4.0, https://commons.wikimedia.orgwindex.phpcurid=89795018)

against the German defenses supported by the 1st Guards Rifle Corps. Within a few hours advanced elements of the 63rd Rifle Corps had punched a hole in the German line, pouring troops through the breach. The 10th Rifle Corps then exploited this and quickly gained ground. The Red Army Air Force too supported the infantry attacks, strafing and bombing as German troops withdrew from one shattered position to another. The Luftwaffe did what they could, but their fighter force was overstretched and ineffective.

By May 6, the Germans had sustained some 5,000 casualties, and the ring around Sevastopol was on the point of cracking. Throughout the day the Soviets applied continuous pressure against the German defenses, hoping to achieve a breakthrough. Unabated fighting continued through the night and throughout the rest of the following day with the Germans trying to contain the overwhelming might of the Red Army. German infantry positions comprising artillery, antitank, and heavy and light machine guns were entrenched in the Sapun Hills—regarded as the gateway to Sevastopol from the south. Allmendinger had sent explicit orders to his battered troops to hold out as long as possible. It was not to be. Securing the heights allowed the Red Army a clear field of fire over the entire vista as far down to the tip of Cape Khersones. Fighting spilled out across the heights with the Germans trying in vain to regain the high ground.

There is a wealth of detail in this image. Soviet troops along the bay at Sevastopol following its capture. An abandoned German Sturmgeschütz III is in the foreground. Much of the German heavy armor was either destroyed or left behind.

On the beach near Sevastopol is a Soviet naval officer armed with a PPSh-41 submachine gun. Hurrying behind him is a Maxim 1910 machine-gun crew.

Wounded German POWs in Sevastopol, early May. Their future is bleak.

The following day, May 8, the 63rd Rifle Corps managed to successfully dislodge the remaining German defenses. The 10th Rifle Corps was then ordered to pour its forces through the breach toward Sevastopol. Despite a German counterattack, the Soviets were too powerful. Allmendinger reported that it was almost impossible to hold any position around Sevastopol. He was also concerned that with the deteriorating situation his troops would soon be compelled to fight inside the port itself where his army would certainly be annihilated. Even Schörner, Hitler's Eastern Front defense expert, was under no illusion as to the seriousness of the Soviet breach. He sent a message to Führer headquarters: "Request evacuation since further defense of Sevastopol no longer possible." During the early hours of May 9, Hitler, not wanting to experience another Stalingrad, finally agreed to the evacuation.

Already the port of Sevastopol was under heavy bombardment with troops now trying to withdraw to Cape Khersones to save themselves. Luckily for the Germans the deep trenches and concrete fortifications protected many. The narrow front hindered the Soviet assaults, and divisional attacks could only be launched piecemeal.

The evacuation of the Crimea was codenamed Operation *60,000*. Since April 15, various German and Romanian warships had been escorting convoys between Constanta and Sevastopol supplying the peninsula. The last phase of the operation was the evacuation of troops from Sevastopol. On May 11, with renewed Soviet assaults, Allmendinger desperately appealed to Admiral Otto Schulz, the German naval commander, to evacuate his men or they would face destruction. That night the general gave the order for all units to fall back to the coast and dig in at predetermined landing points to await the ships. However, some boats had to turn back to Constanta empty, while others only took on board a fraction of the troops they could carry. According to the navy, the whole cape was shrouded in smoke from the Soviet shelling. The Soviets had also sent in smoke drums to hinder visibility. As a result, a massive smokescreen obscured the docks and landing areas, and the boats were unable to get close inshore. Frantic messages were sent from the Seventeenth Army. Some boats attempted the perilous evacuation, many others did not. The result was chaos. Of the 64,700 men on the Crimea during the first week of May, 26,700 were left behind to fall into Soviet hands. Although most German troops escaped from the Crimea, Tolbukhin was furious that they had managed to be evacuated. He immediately ordered that his troops quell the remaining German units left behind with tanks and infantry. The Germans were helpless. When the Soviets captured the remaining Germans, an eyewitnesses recalled Soviet officers ordering their troops to line up German soldiers and shoot them.

Dejected and wounded German POWs await their fate. All are shoeless.

A lengthy column of German POWs trudge along a dusty road in the Cape of Khersones, May 1944.

Soviet troops survey the equipment and detritus of war left behind by the Germans and Romanians during their evacuation.

In Profile:
Soviet Sailors

Independent Coastal Army, 2nd Guards Rifle Division, 11th Guards Rifle Corps, 4th Ukrainian Front, Sevastopol, May 9, 1944

Soviet sailors in Sevastopol in the traditional seaman's uniform. Sailors were issued a black, flat-topped M24 *bezkozirka*, the seaman's cap, and a black *pilotka* garrison cap. (Renato Dalmaso)

Independent Coastal Army, 55th Guards Rifle Division, 20th Guards Rifle Corps, 4th Ukrainian Front, Sevastopol, May 9, 1944

A sailor belonging to the Black Sea Fleet raises the Soviet flag over Sevastopol following its recapture. (Renato Dalmaso)

Aftermath

In the evacuation of the Crimea, it took four days to remove the German and Romanian forces that were hemmed in and isolated along Cape Khersones. The evacuation was perilous and chaotic, but in the aftermath Admiral Otto Schulz and Rear Admiral Horia Macellariu, the Black Sea naval commander of the Crimea, were awarded the Knight's Cross of the Iron Cross. As for Generals Jaenecke and Allmendinger, Hitler ordered that they were never to receive another command until a court-martial determined what he called "the suspicion that all was not done that might have been done to hold the Crimea."

The Soviet Crimean offensive had been a complete disaster for the German Army: some 31,700 Germans and 25,800 Romanians were killed in battle or wounded. Over 20,000 were lost in action and almost 10,000 captured. According to Stavka reports the Red Army put their losses at 84,331 killed or wounded.

The numbers killed and wounded in the Crimea can be attributed to Hitler's insistence on fanatically ordering the Seventeenth Army to hold every inch of ground when the peninsula was no longer of strategic importance. However, Hitler blamed the loss of the Crimea not on the overwhelming strength of the enemy and the fact that both the Axis forces were cut off but held Jaenecke and Allmendinger responsible for not defending the peninsula.

As for the Soviets, the liberation of the Crimea was a great success, despite the fact the many thousands of enemy soldiers had managed to evade capture by being evacuated by sea. Stavka had not been in any real rush to take the Crimea. One Soviet officer who had been interrogating a captured German officer openly admitted to him that "we were in no hurry to take the Crimea. After all, it was our biggest POW cage. The Germans were virtually prisoners on the peninsula since November 1943. They guarded themselves. They supplied themselves. They went on leave and even returned by their own account."

The reverberations caused by the loss of the Crimea had little effect on the way operations were fought out during the summer of 1944 on the Eastern Front. Strategically, the Wehrmacht was already withdrawing through the Ukraine while the Red Army hounded them. Even before the Crimean offensive was launched in April, Stavka were drawing up plans for a massive summer offensive—Operation *Bagration*—to annihilate German Army Group Center. The offensive would be so destructive it would disrupt the whole German position in southern Russia and the Ukraine on a magnitude far greater than any other Soviet offensive launched to date. Despite the deteriorating situation west of the Dnieper River, and growing intelligence reports of a new Soviet summer offensive looming, Hitler remained obsessed with holding on to the Crimea. He told his war staff that the peninsula was of great strategic importance because of the Romanian oil refineries and the iron and manganese mines at Krivoi Rog and Nikopol. The Soviets, however, saw the Crimean offensive as a side show. The day Hitler ordered the Seventeenth Army onto the peninsula he inadvertently sealed their fate and deprived the Eastern Front of vital men and equipment.

Further Reading

Bork, Bruno. *StuG III Brigade 191, 1940–1945: The Buffalo Brigade in Action in the Balkans, Greece and from Moscow to Kursk and Sevastopol.* London: Greenhill Books, 2021.

Clark, Alan. *Barbarossa: The Russian-German Conflict, 1941–1945.* New York: HarperCollins Publishing, Inc., 1965.

Donnell, Clayton. *The Defence of Sevastopol 1941–1942: The Soviet Perspective.* Barnsley: Pen & Sword Military, 2016.

Erickson, John. *The Road to Stalingrad: Stalin's War with Germany.* New Haven: Yale University Press, 1975.

Glantz, David M., and Jonathan House. *When Titans Clashed: How the Red Army Stopped Hitler.* Lawrence: University Press of Kansas, 1995.

Harrison, Richard W. *The Russian Way of War: Operational Art, 1904–1940.* Lawrence: University Press of Kansas, 2001.

Menning, Bruce W. "Operation Art's Origins," *Military Review*, 77, No. 5 (September October). Ft. Leavenworth: Army Combined Arms Center, 1997.

Palmer, R. R., Joel Colton, and Lloyd Kramer. *A History of the Modern World.* New York: McGraw-Hill, 2002.

Paret, Peter, and Gordon A. Craig, et al. *Makers of Modern Strategy from Machiavelli to the Nuclear Age.* New Jersey: Princeton University Press, 1986.

Pinter, Walter, and Peter Paret, (ed.). *The Making of Soviet Strategy in Makers of Modern Strategy.* New Jersey: Princeton University Press, 1986.

Porter, Bruce. *War and the Rise of the State.* New York: Macmillan, 1994.

Tucker-Jones, Anthony. *Stalin's Armour, 1941–1945: Soviet Tanks at War.* Barnsley: Pen & Sword Military, 2021.

Tucker-Jones, Anthony. *The Battle for the Crimea 1941–1944.* Barnsley: Pen & Sword Military, 2016.

Wade, John. *Cameras at War: Photo Gear that Captured 100 Years of Conflict—From Crimea to Korea.* Barnsley: Pen & Sword Military, 2020.

Ziemke, Earl. *Stalingrad to Berlin: The German Defeat in the East.* Washington D.C.: Center of Military History, United States Army.

Index